MAGIC IN ISLAM

Michael
Muhammad Knight

MAGIC IN ISLAM

A TarcherPerigee Book

tarcherperigee

TarcherPerigee
An imprint of Penguin Random House LLC
375 Hudson Street
New York, New York 10014

Library of Congress Cataloging-in-Publication Data

Names: Knight, Michael Muhammad, author.
Title: Magic in Islam / Michael Muhammad Knight.
Description: New York : TarcherPerigee / 2016. | Includes bibliographical references.
Identifiers: LCCN 2015048273 (print) | LCCN 2015049295 (ebook)
ISBN 9780399176708 (hardcover) | ISBN 9781101983492 (ebook)
Subjects: LCSH: Magic—Religious aspects—Islam. | Islamic magic.
BISAC: BODY, MIND & SPIRIT / Magick Studies. | RELIGION / Islam / General. | RELIGION / Mysticism. Classification: LCC BP190.5.M25 K58 2016 (print) | LCC BP190.5.M25 (ebook)
DDC 297.3/9—dc23

Printed in the United States of America
1 3 5 7 9 10 8 6 4 2

Book design by Elke Sigal

For Azreal, teacher and friend

Contents

1

Introducing Muslim Magic

They said, "You are only of those affected by magic."
—QUR'ĀN 26:153

This project began with interest in a genre of literature that has proliferated in American publishing, particularly in the years following 9/11: the "intro to Islam." Designed to provide the non-Muslim reader with basic awareness of Muslim beliefs and practices, these introductions deal in glimpses from afar. They zoom their lenses all the way out, offering Islam as it might look from light-years away. These introductions can serve a useful purpose, since Americans don't score high on cultural literacy; but the genre itself comes with pluses and minuses.

The constraints of the "intro" genre, regardless of the specific topic, require that the author create the topic anew, because the author must take vast amounts of material and complexity and boil it all down to what s/he considers to be the essential concepts and information for a reader with no prior familiarity. Given the immeasurable diversity of Muslim beliefs, interpretations, practices, and communities even in our present world, not to mention Muslim diversity throughout nearly fifteen centuries, writing an introduction to Islam means that the author must locate some workable center. Works in this genre often attempt to ground their material in things like the text of the Qur'ān (believed to be the word of God as revealed to Muḥammad), the corpus of *ḥadīth* literature (statements and actions attributed to Muḥammad), and generalized ideas about belief and practice, constructing Islam through a bulleted set of key points. The intro books typically present Islam as resting upon a scriptural foundation, scriptural which isn't necessarily *wrong*—plenty of Muslims would agree with this depiction—but reflects the choices of their authors and the often Protestant-ish assumptions about religion that inform the genre at large. They give us Islam as defined by scripture (and "scripture" as they choose to define it), theologians, and jurists while all but abstracted from history, with little sense that the prescriptive works of Islam's seminal thinkers do not necessarily reflect Islam as lived on the ground, in the experience of real human bodies. I can't imagine Islam as only a tradition made only by the books that defeated other books in power struggles to become canon. There are also the intellectuals of the past who, for whatever reason, failed to become authoritative for later generations. When we leave them out of our intro books, we present Islam as an unchanging thing that exists outside of time, rather than as the site of contests between competing forces with different ideas about what constitutes the authentic and authoritative, with not a singular canon but a multiplicity of canons that can both oppose and overlap one another.

We should also consider that before modern printing and increases in literacy, these brilliant premodern intellectuals—the winners and losers, privileged and suppressed voices alike—typically wrote with neither the ability nor the interest in communicating with the masses, but were more often elitists arguing with other elitists. What about the vast majority of Muslims throughout the centuries who left no books behind, and whose lived experiences of the tradition would be dismissed or outright condemned by the elite thinkers? The intro-to-Islam genre does not tend to take them seriously as participants and contributors.

Other elements in these books and their organizational structures reveal the authors' often unspoken beliefs and priorities: relegating Shī'ism or Ṣūfism to their own separate chapters, for example, rather than a more integrated approach that includes these traditions within Islam at large; emphasis on Islamic law and theories of the state; narratives of Muslims' intellectual or civilizational "decline," attempts at "renewal," and related crises of "Islam in the modern world";[1] separate chapters on women, as though Muslim women only show up at a particular moment in history (that is, when Europeans and Americans become aware of them as a symbol of civilizational difference); or a chapter in *The Beliefnet Guide to Islam* titled "The Sum of All Fears: Freedom, Jihad, and Gender."[2] This should be obvious and go without saying, but the selection of chapters and topics reveals the priorities of the author, rather than simply Islam as it is.

Deciding what's crucial for a basic or introductory glance at Islam also means deciding what we can afford to leave out and cut away: whatever texts, practices, traditions, communities, and *people* are minor, marginal, and unnecessary. By presenting what s/he has judged to be essential knowledge, the author of the intro genre does not simply privilege the mainstream, but *invents* it. Perhaps it should not be a surprise, then, that these intro-to-Islam books, providing the "basic information" as defined by the authors, the anticipated needs of readers, and the desires of the publishing industry, focus on topics of modernity, violence, liberal democracy, religious pluralism, and the "women in Islam" question. And these books don't have room for chapters on magic.

Surrounded by introductions to Islam that cannot help but become productions *of* Islam, I had to wonder how an intro to Islam might look if written from a completely different set of priorities. Perhaps an introduction to Islam could depart from other works in the genre by not locating Islam's center in a supposed "heartland" of Arab nations, but instead looking at places with higher populations of Muslims—nations such as Indonesia, Nigeria, Turkey, Iran, Pakistan, and even India (where India's Muslim communities, generally estimated at below 20 percent of the overall population, numerically overwhelm Saudi Arabia's 99 percent Muslim population). One could write an introduction to Islam that was not Sunnī-centered, or male-centered, or law-centered, or faithful to a predetermined canon; what would an introduction to Islam look like if it did not let only the classical male theologians and jurists speak, but let the intro come through marginalized voices? Add them up and they become the mainstream.

What if someone wrote an introduction to Islam for general readers in which magic became the primary lens that informed the author's priorities? If all introductions are inescapably *productive*, what kind of "Islam" would that produce?

Creeping Mageia

Before getting into Islam's possible relationships to magic, we have to decide what the word "magic" even means, which is more complicated than one might expect. Magic makes for a slippery concept. Like "gender," "race," or any other term that can be picked apart as a social construction—which of course means *all* of our terms, every attempt at producing order through language and classification—the word "magic" does not simply express a straightforward, self-evident reality, but rather creative reimaginings on the part of everyone who uses it. Magic's meaning is continually shaped and reshaped by changes in our knowledge, values, and prejudices. Scholars writing about magic today, when confronted with the matter of definitions, often choose to simply admit the incoherence and uselessness of the topic and then move forward with their projects.[3] If I can name a book *Magic in Islam* without having to say what exactly belongs in the category of "magic," this will be my approach as well.

Our operational definitions of magic often emerge through deciding what magic is *not*, particularly in relation to two other slippery concepts: religion and science. Presented as separate from religion, magic becomes simply an inferior version of religion, powerless at best and demonic at worst. In similar fashion, science attains the full prestige of "science" in part while representing magic (and often religion) as its primitive and irrational ancestor. The idea of religion and science as irreconcilably separate from each other positions magic as a scorned third space, marginalized by both. Religionists concerned with proving their rationalism and compatibility with science often make efforts to separate their religions from anything magical, while many pro-science atheist thinkers charge that any distinction between religion and magic is flimsy at best. Some would even mock religion by tagging it with vocabularies of magic: *hocus-pocus*, *witchcraft*, *spells*. In both religious and scientific contexts, "magic" becomes a slur.

The problem for a "magic in Islam" project, however, is that these relationships are not remotely stable: like magic itself, they move and change. What one community regards as mere superstition would be another community's divinely revealed or empirically observed knowledge. In many settings, the categories of religion, science, and magic blur into each other with little hope for authoritatively distinguishing one from the others. When we try to write about these relationships across history, presuming that religion, science, and magic have always existed in the forms in which we presently recognize them, the results tend to say more about us than about the categories themselves.

Like so many of our categories of analysis, magic as a concept can be traced back to Europeans exoticizing, fetishizing, and fearing cultural difference. It starts as an ancient version of Orientalism: The term "magic" derives from the Greek *mageia*, which was taken from the Persian *magav* and first used in reference to Persian priests, who were regarded as skilled dream interpreters and astrologers. According to Herodotus, these priests (*magos*, *magoi*) consulted famed kings such as Xerxes, accompanied the sacred fire on military campaigns, and were required for certain ritual acts during sacrifices.[4] The label united suspicion of the foreign with anxieties regarding the supernatural. Mageia conjured images of a distant land of strange customs, the looming threat of the Persian Empire—a dominant military superpower in its time—and arcane technologies by which priests could communicate with gods and access incalculable power.

Central to the Greek narrative of mageia was the figure of Zarathustra, whose renaming in Greek as "Zoroastres"—including *aster*, the Greek word for star—encouraged his rebranding in European imagination as a powerful astrologer.[5] Though the exact positions of the priests remain sources of scholarly debate,[6] the Greek conception of mageia bore associations with the religious tradition that we would now call Zoroastrianism. In Persia, priests were identified with *magav* or variants of the term until the rise of Islam and end of the Sasanian Empire; the Qur'ān refers to Zoroastrians as *al-Majūs*.[7]

Greek literatures, expanding mageia beyond Persian priestcraft, gradually came to associate the term with any practice that sought to manipulate unseen forces, as well as the false claims to such abilities by hucksters and con artists. "To an Ionian of the late sixth century BCE," writes Fritz Graf, "a *magos* was not so much a wizard as a ritual specialist on the margins of society, with wide-ranging functions, ridiculed by some, secretly dreaded by others."[8] In Sophocles's *Oedipus Rex*, Oedipus condemns Creon as "this *magos* hatcher of plots, this crafty begging priest."[9]

The magos/magus was also vulnerable to prosecution as a criminal. In his *Apology*, Numidian Berber writer Apuleius (ca. 124–170 CE) employs the terms' multiplicity of meanings as part of his legal defense. Charged with mageia as a criminal act, Apuleius draws a distinction between mageia as Zoroaster's system of knowledge and piety (in which identifying Apuleius as a magus only meant that he was a priest) and popular distortions, which would associate mageia with self-serving incantations.[10] The Hellenic Jewish intellectual Philo (25 BCE–50 CE) likewise observes a clear difference between authentic Persian mageia, which he considers an established science of priests and kings, and "the counterfeit of this, most properly called an evil art," which he associates with the ignorant practices of "altar parasites," slaves, and women. The difference is crucial, Philo argues, in understanding Moses's order to expel diviners and execute practitioners of mageia.[11] Apuleius and Philo might be read as offering premodern versions of the religion-magic opposition, but writing on the genealogy of magic, J. N. Bremmer warns against imposing these categories onto the ancient Mediterranean. Even as numerous Greek writers, both pre- and post-Christian, argued over the propriety of incantations, formulas, and other practices, they did not do so within a clear binary of magic vs. religion: "two terms and concepts, which did not exist in antiquity, but are both the product of late- and post-medieval Europe."[12]

Zoroaster's prestige transcended categories that we might attempt to inscribe upon the past. As Zoroaster and his priesthood were imagined as originators and custodians of ancient and exotic knowledge, Greek literatures portrayed Pythagoras, Empedocles, Democritus, and Plato as all having studied mageia in the East.[13] Apuleius believed that Pythagoras had personally learned under Zoroaster himself; in the Roman era, Pliny the Elder would confidently assert that *magicus* originated "in Persia with Zoroaster."[14] As the long-gone historical person of Zoroaster grew into a celebrity brand associated with exotic "alien wisdoms" and ancient knowledge, Greek authors appropriated him for their own authorization, attributing new treatises of philosophy, astrology, alchemy, and history to his pen.[15]

Writers could even borrow Zoroaster's prestige to glorify a new savior: this is what we see in the Gospel of Matthew, when Christ's birth is marked by his visit from magi who recognize and affirm his status. Originating from an unspecified "East," these magi traveled to Jerusalem and then Bethlehem to worship the awaited King of the Jews. How did they know that the Messiah was about to appear? By observing his star in the night sky. Muḥammad's Christian contemporary Isidore of Seville (ca. 560–636) names Zoroaster as the originator of magic and recognizes the magi as the first astrologers, but clarifies, "Knowledge of this skill was permitted only up until the time of the Gospel, so that once Christ was born no one thereafter would interpret the birth of anyone from the heavens."[16] The identity of the magi shifted with the centuries: when Muslim empires dominated the Mediterranean, European Christians Africanized one of the magi, popularly named Balthasar, as a "Moor." Today, the popular English translation of magi as simply "wise men" might erase the original significance of these characters, but I'm guessing that Christ's endorsement by Zoroastrian priestly astrologers could present challenges for the Gospel's modern readers.

Throughout antiquity and medieval Europe, we find Christians doing things that might fit into *our* definitions of magic, engaging in folk healing, amulets, talismans, various forms of divination, and incantations. In early Christian Egypt, for example, monastery archives sometimes included what could be called magical spells, recipes that employed prayers to the Persons of the Trinity with fragments from mummies' bodies.[17] We also find Christians opposing such practices for their perceived associations with paganism, heresy, demons, or as attempts to transgress divinely placed limits on human knowledge. Astrology notably falls in and out of (and *back* into) Christian favor, between Augustine's condemnation and a later Christianized zodiac. But if premodern Christian Europe did not yet have our modern separation of magic and religion, what could the label of "magic" have signified? While there are cases of ritual practitioners in the Greco-Egyptian context and elsewhere referencing magic as part of their self-identification, magic usually functioned as what Kimberly B. Stratton calls a "discourse of alterity . . . conveying ideas of Otherness and marginality," expressing a perceived "weirdness factor."[18] Just as many people today use the term "cult" to dismiss religious communities that they find offensive, illegitimate, absurd, or dangerous, "magic" worked as a premodern label of marginalization and disavowal. Christian arguments used the category of magic to separate genuine miracles of holy people from the deceitful tricks of imposters and the dark arts of Satan, or to distinguish between competing objects of worship and veneration. The line drawn by Christian thinkers such as Augustine between religion and magic could be reassessed as a line between different modes of religion, arguing on behalf of Christianity against whatever was marked as outside its limits. This mode of boundary-drawing also took place between Christians: while the Catholic Church denounced pagan rituals as magic and portrayed Jewish rabbis as Satanic wizards, its Protestant opponents would redirect that same charge against Catholic rituals. Reformation-era polemics against Catholicism commonly mocked belief in Christ's presence in the Eucharist as mere magic, while denouncing priests as crude magicians.

The Christian crisis of the Reformation, along with increasing engagement of cultures beyond Christian-Jewish-Muslim milieus in the Age of Exploration, contributed toward the development of "religion" as a category. "Magic" materialized as a separate entity from "religion" alongside the notion of a religion as a codified system of belief (and the newly recognized possibility of *religions* existing in the plural). The European study of religions in modernity, as filtered through Euro-Christian frameworks and prejudices, gave us a number of terms that can be easily historicized and deconstructed, but which we tend to take for granted as expressing empirically observed, concrete realities: "animism," "shamanism," "mysticism," "gnosticism," and of course "magic" and "religion" themselves.

In the age of colonial domination, European scholars constructed magic and religion as relating to each other on an imaginary timeline of human progress that, incidentally, privileged Europe. British anthropologist E. B. Tylor (1832–1917) argues in *Primitive Culture* that the lost prehistories of "modern cultured nations" can be understood through study of "lower races," since the lower races represent earlier stages of the higher races' evolution. The persistence of magical beliefs among higher races, being a "survival" from their primitive pasts, can thus be examined through considering the place of magic among lower races.[19] In his classic volume *The Golden Bough*, British anthropologist James G. Frazer (1854–1941) argues that magic precedes religion in human development as a primitive attempt at science ("the bastard sister of science"), only to be later replaced by religion, which in turn gets replaced by real science. In Frazer's narrative, magic had originated as an attempt to achieve control over nature. As societies mature to realize that magic cannot fulfill its promises, they progress toward religion. For Frazer, the journey out of magic thus distinguishes the developed mind from the primitive. As "civilized races" graduate from magic to religion, they leave "savages" behind: "Roughly speaking, all [aboriginal] men in Australia are magicians, but not one is a priest."[20] In Frazer's view, religion differs from magic in that religion does not seek control over impersonal forces of nature, but rather offers a means to win the favor of gods who can control nature on behalf of human beings. After religion, Frazer's next phase of human development arrives with the ascent of science. Like magic and unlike religion, science recognizes that nature is impersonal; unlike both magic and religion, science comprehends how nature really works.

Randall Styers observes that changing ideas about "magic" engaged European anxieties about science and modernity, and argues that these evolutionary models served an unfortunate ideological purpose. The academic separation of magic from religion bolstered the confidence of rationalized European Protestants in their own cultural and racial superiority. Presenting magic, religion, and science as distinct stops along the march of civilizational progress affirmed the right—even the *duty*—of "advanced" scientific nations to invade and colonize magical peoples who had failed to properly develop. "Theories of magic confirmed that the mental processes of nonmodern, non-Western peoples are benighted and superstitious," Styers writes. "A propensity to magic demonstrates an incapacity for responsible self-government; people prone to magic call out for enlightened control."[21] Frazer himself acknowledges his sources of the magic-religion binary as Sir Alfred Lyall (1835–1911), a colonial administrator in India who contrasted Indian magic against "the religion of civilization," and historian Frank Jevons (1858–1936), who identified magic as the system of "less civilized" peoples and religion as that of the "more civilized."[22] The sharpened division of religion and magic, and the question of which traditions and communities fit into each category, were inescapably bound in developing ideas about race and the myth of the "white man's burden."

The irony is that while racist white men cited "primitive" belief in magic as part of the rationale for their dominance over the rest of the world, a new renaissance of magic was flourishing within Western empires (much to Tylor's dismay). The Euro-American magic revival emerged in large part as a product of the colonial encounter, which produced new imaginaries of a fantastical, mystical, enchanted "East" and revisited classical Hellenic associations of magic with the foreign and exotic. The resurgent Orientalism of Western magic might have been exemplified in Harry Houdini wearing a turban and the clothes of a "Hindu fakir" at the 1893 World's Fair in Chicago as he claimed to perform "Indian magic," and the first American magazine for professional magicians launching in 1895 with the title *Mahatma*.

This racializing and Orientalizing of magic holds consequences for today's world, as societies that take magic seriously are still imagined to deserve benevolent invasion and occupation. While the criminalization of witchcraft can be found in numerous countries, it is the appearance of such laws in Muslim-majority countries that most easily captures American imagination. Stories of Muslims fearing magic preserve the image of Islam as fundamentally irrational and inescapably "medieval," a relic of another time that cannot catch up to the rest of the world. For the Saudi state to prosecute witchcraft as an act of real violence would prove, in the eyes of many outside observers, the urgent need to reform Islam—perhaps through military intervention—to make Muslims more compatible with the "modern" world. This ignores the persistence of anti-magic laws in non-Muslim-majority countries such as India, Cameroon, or the United Kingdom. The UK's

Witchcraft Act of 1736, which prohibited conjure and "dealing with evil and wicked Spirits," was eventually supplanted by the Fraudulent Mediums Act, which repositioned contact with spirits as a matter of deception rather than genuine demonic power; this repeal/rewrite only took place in 1951. In my own state of North Carolina, it remains a Class 2 misdemeanor to "practice the arts of phrenology, palmistry, clairvoyance, fortune-telling and other crafts of a similar kind."[23] Beyond states' criminalization of magic, vigilante and mob violence against accused practitioners can be found on every continent, committed by adherents of every religion and no religion.

Looking historically at the construction of magic, what we end up with is not a coherent definition or theory but rather a troubling sense of how the label has been used repeatedly to designate beliefs, practices, or entire cultures as foreign, strange, exotic, demonic, heretical, ignorant, irrational, and anti-modern. When belief in magic is used to paint these pictures, excited media coverage over the Saudi government establishing anti-witchcraft police units feeds into a larger "Clash of Civilizations" narrative. Obviously, the service of magic to this narrative is only possible when we choose to ignore the persistence of magical beliefs and practices in the United States and Europe throughout the twentieth century and into the twenty-first, exemplified less in government persecution of witches than in thriving capitalist enterprises of magic-centered books, Web sites, products, and services.

Translation always brings a threat to the translated. I'm writing a book about magic in Islam with a particular vocabulary, starting with the obvious fact that I write in English. The epigraph that opens this chapter, presenting the Qur'ān in English translation, presents the word "magic" as corresponding to a concept within the revealed text. Many Muslim writers, scholars, and preachers who work in English will refer to "magic" without ever interrogating the term, as though we could find a literal match for the English "magic" and its exact range of meanings within the texts of Muslim intellectual tradition—even though the word "magic" isn't even consistent in its own language across time and space. But that's not how language works; to speak of "magic" brings a particular genealogy to our conversation. The question may not be what the Qur'ān says about magic, but whether it *can* speak on magic at all.

Consider the edited volume *Defining Magic: A Reader*, which explores the conceptual genealogy of magic through a collection of historical primary sources as well as scholarly literature. Scanning through the included authors—Plato, Pliny the Elder, Plotinus, Augustine, Thomas Aquinas, Helena Petrovna Blavatsky, and modern academics such as E. B. Tylor, Sir James George Frazer, Marcel Mauss, Henri Hubert, and Émile Durkheim—it becomes apparent that *Defining Magic* deals with magic as essentially a European concept that comes to us through European history, and to which only European (and later American) scholars could have contributed.[24] Even if many of the European writers were attempting to study or appropriate other cultures, the result nonetheless comes to us as what Europeans saw with their European eyes. As Stratton asserts in the same volume, "What gets labelled magic is arbitrary and depends on the society in question"; we must recognize the limitations of magic as a concept for speaking beyond the histories that produced it.[25] Classical Muslim thinkers such as al-Kindī, Suhrawārdī, al-Ghazālī, Ibn Taymiyya, Ibn al-'Arabī, and Ibn Khaldūn, all of whom had much to say about the technologies that we'd call "magical," were not invited to this conversation. Thirteenth-century philosopher Fākhruddīn al-Rāzī's commentary on the Qur'ān includes a taxonomy of different sciences and practices within the category of *siḥr*, the Qur'ān's term that we commonly translate as "magic" or "sorcery" today: these included not only expected items such as astrology, the achievement of spectacular acts through the help of spirits and demons, and even juggling and sleight-of-hand deceptions, but also the use of drugs and perfumes to confuse people, the charismatic seduction of crowds, and causing divisions between people through slander and spreading rumors.[26] Does this all add up to match our category of "magic"? What about practices that we might call magic, but that al-Rāzī has excluded from his list? Al-Rāzī's construction of siḥr draws from various intellectual genealogies, including Hellenic traditions and Muslim ḥadīth reports, statements attributed to Muḥammad. Al-Rāzī, however, is not seen as a conversation partner for contemporary Western scholars who want to write about magic, which makes for a problem when writing in English about magic in Islam. Without pretending that a separate "Muslim world" exists in complete isolation from the "West," writing about magic in Islam still presents the problem of imagining a European concept as global.

If we don't like "magic," there are alternatives, but every label has the potential to create new challenges. So it is with esotericism and the occult: "esoteric" comes from the Greek *esoterikos*, meaning "the inner," while "occult" comes from the Latin *occulto*, "to hide, keep secret." What might serve as a loose Islamic equivalent for the esoteric, the Arabic *bāṭin*, brings unique historical baggage: as medieval Muslim communities engaged in sectarian polemics against each other, the label of *bāṭinī* functioned as a Sunnī slur against Ismā'īlī Shī'īs (as well as some Ṣūfīs and philosophers), who were accused of rejecting the Qur'ān's clear, plain-sense content in favor of their leaders' claims to have uncovered the scripture's hidden meanings. In an Islamic studies context, to discuss "esotericism" as an alternative to "magic" additionally forces us to reconsider the boundary between esoteric/magical material and mysticism, which blows the project wide open. Attempting to determine where magic begins and mysticism ends, or position mysticism between two subjective categories of magic and religion—as with our boundaries between magic and religion or magic and science—only reveals the flimsiness of our constructs. The Arabic *ghayb*, signifying the secret or hidden, also links to specific references in Muslim traditions, as the Qur'ān refers to an *al-ghayb* that is known only to Allāh and is beyond the limits of human knowledge.[27] There is also the Shī'ī concept of *ghayba*, which describes the status of the Imām who has withdrawn from the world and exists in a metaphysical stasis through the centuries until his awaited return. *Ghayba* often appears in translation as "occultation," but I am not convinced that this gives us an easy entrance into thinking about a "Muslim occult."

"Esotericism" as a unit of analysis developed in nineteenth-century Europe at a time when post-Enlightenment thought continued its break from establishment Christianity; according to Guy G. Stroumsa, use of "Esoterisme" traces back to Jacques Matter's 1828 work *Histoire du gnosticisme.*[28] Similarly, the "occult" as a concept emerges fairly recently—"Before the late eighteenth century," writes Paul Kléber Monod, "the idea of the 'occult' would not have made much sense to speakers of English"; Monod adds that "occultism" as an organized category emerges post-1875 and imposes modern ideas and structure onto diverse and disorganized earlier materials.[29] As these modern categories would find increasing currency, esotericism/occultism came to represent a coherent premodern body of subcultures and traditions that had struggled underground throughout the ages to survive against suppressive church power. This narrative oversimplifies European intellectual and religious histories, and I won't try to retrieve it for use in analyzing Muslim traditions.

In contemporary sources, the notion of historical esotericism or occultism might be employed to claim a history that stands entirely *outside* Christianity or in opposition to it. Such a separation can serve an ideological purpose for Christians who wish to purge their faith of ideas and behaviors that they find dangerous, as well as for contemporary self-identified esotericists who desire a countertradition that can stand in resistance against organized religion. This approach is of limited usefulness. Even if a clear division between Christianity and the magical/esoteric/occult might be favored by many on both sides of that binary, we also have to consider the ways in which each side informs and defines the other, as well as those who did not perceive a division at all. The problem with identifying occultism in European Christian contexts also tells us something about a "Muslim occult."

The ways that we speak of magic, esotericism, or the occult in relation to Islam could imply that these things should not be regarded as organic elements *within* Muslim traditions. Depending on your personal investments, you might treat these materials as alien intrusions that threaten to corrupt Islam from outside, or as sources of a superior wisdom that Muslims have alternately sought to suppress or plagiarize, but could never legitimately claim as their own. Both sides might treat "Islamic magic" not as legitimately Islamic but inescapably Greek, Persian, Indian, Central Asian, or West African, forever the result of an alien textual tradition, local shamanism, or confused "syncretism" disguising itself as Islam. This project's intention is not to run a DNA test on Islamic magic to prove that Islam is or is not this baby's father; my interest does not lie in acting as the guardian of an "orthodox Islam," whatever that might mean, nor in liberating some Great Secret from an imagined orthodoxy's strictures.

Certainly, not every "occult" practitioner who worked within a Christian or Jewish context would have self-identified as Christian or Jewish; likewise, not every occultist working within a Muslim context necessarily regarded his/her materials as harmonious with Islam. But plenty of them *did*: throughout history, we find committed Christians, Jews, and Muslims casting spells, consulting spirits, and making use of astrology, sometimes to prove the truth of their faith convictions. Furthermore, such practices often appear to be far from "marginal," but feature prominently in these traditions *as lived by the people who claim them*. The truth is that in Christian, Jewish, and Muslim traditions, much of what we might call "magical" practices were (and are) often at least as popular and publicly accessible as the forces that condemned them, and often more so. If the occult is mainstream, what's "occult" about it?

So this is where we end up: (1) the term "magic" is not all that useful; (2) deciding where "Muslim religion" ends and "Muslim magic" begins (as with the division between religion and magic in Jewish, Christian, Buddhist, or Hindu traditions) has more to do with our personal prejudices about what constitutes "authentic" or "orthodox" religion than any characteristics inherent to the things themselves; (3) to rely on "magic" as a meaningful category of analysis, even if you're writing about non-European contexts, could mean that you insist on living in a Europe-centered universe; (4) replacing "magic" with terms such as "esotericism" or "the occult" doesn't help. Closer examination of these artifacts undermines not only the coherence of magic/esotericism/occultism as a topic, but Islam and religion more broadly—which brings us to our next problem.

How Not to Write About Religion

Every so often, an irritating image shows up in my social media feeds: "The Evolutionary Tree of Myth and Religion," credited to designer Simon E. Davies.[30] As the title suggests, the chart purports to display how the world's significant religious traditions relate to each other, using a family tree model and chronicling their "evolution." It seems that many people in my social media worlds consider the tree project to be comprehensive and well researched, but the results are naïve, patronizing, and racist. The various branches of the tree are color-coded by their geographical origins: Islam, Christianity, and Judaism all appear on the yellow branch, which designates them as religions of the "Middle East." (An earlier version of the tree more clearly racialized this branch as "Semitic.") Despite the obvious expansions of these traditions beyond their origins, Davies's tree locks them forever into the Middle East as though their geographic roots express something innate and unchanging about them. (Again, consider that the previous version framed this not as geographic, but explicitly racial.)

Davies's own investments and priorities are clear in his hyper-detailed treatment of European religious diversity, both premodern and modern, compared to his utter negligence of other regions, such as Africa and South Asia. On the green European branch, we find Germanic, Slavic, Baltic, Celtic, Norse, and Greek (with numerous offshoots, including Greco-Roman, Hermetic, Hellenic, and Neo-Platonic) polytheisms, leading to modern traditions of Ásatrú, Rodnovery, Romuva, Neo-Druidism, Wicca, Thelema, Rosicrucianism, Theosophy, Golden Dawn, and Anthroposophy. Africa (the brown branch) only gets a primordial division between Berber and Yoruba animisms, followed by Bantu and Nilotic animisms and Ethiopian polytheism; after 900 CE, Africa all but disappears from religion's "evolution," apart from an "African polytheism" that somehow sprouts up at 1550 CE and recognition of African influence through transatlantic slavery on South American and Caribbean movements. Davies makes a place for Egyptian polytheism, but locates it on the Middle Eastern branch, not the African. Of course, neither the European nor African branches contain spaces for Judaism, Christianity, or Islam, since these remain Middle Eastern and cannot be perceived as anything but foreign transplants onto other contexts. Similarly, the South Asian ("Indian") and East Asian branches keep to themselves, nothing going in or out, denying any interactions or exchange between Muslims and Hindus, for example, or Christians and Buddhists. The tree does provide a few dotted lines to indicate influence between branches (more in the revised version than the original), but still preserves these color-coded branches and the categories occupying them as more or less isolated.

Beyond the racializing of religious categories and privileging of modern European movements, the chronological charting of religion's "evolution" produces the most glaring blind spot, because this approach represents each religion as a fixed point in time, defined by its moment of origin. In other words, we get Zoroastrianism at 1100 BCE, Judaism at 950 BCE, Islam at 620 CE, Ṣūfism at 850 CE, and so on. Apart from the question of how Davies chose his dates—is there really a specific moment in 950 BCE at which Judaism suddenly exists?—he fails to account for historical change. For Davies, Judaism is the religion of 950 BCE and always will be, only capable of giving rise to new subbranches (such as Hellenized Judaism or Reformed Judaism). The tree misses the ways in which traditions experience profound *internal* diversity and change that do not usually spawn unique new subbranches. This genetic imaginary of religions relating to each other strictly as parents and children, ancestors and descendants, also leaves out the historical reality of *younger religions influencing and transforming older ones.* This "evolutionary tree," moving in only one direction, fails to chart the ways in which Muslims impacted Zoroastrians, Buddhists affected change in Hindu traditions, and Protestants informed Jewish thought. The tree doesn't allow for a representation of how European conquest transformed religion all over the world, rewriting traditions on European Christian terms (although, according to Davies's tree, there's no such thing as an authentically European Christian). The fact that Davies imagines a fully formed Hinduism existing at 1000 BCE, rather than an extraordinary diversity of traditions that *eventually* crystallize into a construct that bears the English name "Hinduism" in large part through India's *modern* experience of British colonialism, betrays a basic ignorance of how traditions move through time. For many traditions, a more accurate treatment of the religious "tree" would be to turn it upside down. This would show us not a united primordial system that later branches out into "offshoots," but instead the gradual assembling of disparate groups into a standardized "mainstream" or "orthodoxy" that serves to regulate and constrict the limits of diversity.

The "evolutionary" title privileges the most recent developments (again, in the regions where Davies cares about acknowledging them): movements such as Santo Daime, Santería, Hoodoo, Baha'i, Reform Judaism, various Native American shamanisms, and the varied European neo-pagan movements that Davies has extensively detailed. What's missing from the top of religion's evolution? Again, according to Davies, there's nothing new coming out of Africa or Asia. Modern, supposedly monolithic Hinduism has produced a far richer diversity of movements and communities than the various European groups on this tree, but this goes almost entirely undocumented. It is also notable that Davies leaves out movements among Christian, Muslim, Hindu, Buddhist, and other communities that we might brand "fundamentalist." It seems obvious that the Muslim movements and networks that often get labeled as "Salafī" or "Wahhābī" are far more significant in numbers, power, and global presence than any of Davies's favored Euro-pagan revivals, and do much more in defining religion for the twenty-first century—there's no oil-rich Wiccan state that features prominently in U.S. foreign policy interests and promotes its ideology through globalized media networks, as far as I know—but it appears that Davies would imagine these movements as regressions into outdated ancient consciousness, not as new or modern phenomena (and certainly not as contributors to our forward-moving spiritual *evolution*).

Besides the highly selective and inconsistent attention to non-European traditions, these numerous issues might be summed up in one complaint: Davies charts religions as self-contained and stable entities, while neglecting the dynamic and diverse *human communities* that actually exist in history. Proposing to write about magic in Islam, I'd rather avoid the mistakes of evolutionary trees and their guiding assumptions about religion, which are rather popular and widely taken for granted. The historical relationships between these traditions are far too complex and messy to chart in tree form. Though discussion of a religion's relationship to magic could easily uphold that kind of oversimplification—as countless sermons as well as scholarly volumes can demonstrate—I argue that a careful look at magic in Islam cuts the whole tree down. The technologies commonly marked as "magical," as well as the pious oppositions to them, cross all boundaries and become points of encounter between systems that Davies would present as isolated from one another. My hope is that a brief survey of magic in Islam subverts the assumptions in which evolutionary trees are planted.

If there is really a thing in the world that we can name "magic" with any coherence, can there be *Islamic* magic? What would make magic Islamic or un-Islamic—are there different types of magic that can differ from each other in their relationships to Islam? As I am not a theologian or jurist arguing over Islam's true position on magic, I cannot assume any distinction between Islam as a lived tradition on the ground and "Islam" as an abstracted ideal that floats above human cultures. If we have no access to Islam apart from what human beings do with it, then an idea or practice becomes "Islamic" through people identifying it as such, or the term "Islamic" imposes an unnecessary claim of normativity on our materials. Personally, I'd rather call things "Muslim" than "Islamic," valuing the human actors over their possible foundations in real Islam, because I do not speak for real Islam. For similar reasons, by imposing normative judgments on our material, concepts such as "orthodoxy," "heterodoxy," and "syncretism" do more harm than good. These terms operate like magical spells in their own right, employing the power of language to manipulate and reconfigure reality. I'm going to leave them here and keep moving.

Build or Destroy

We've disintegrated "magic" as having the power to meaningfully explain any project, and kicked the legs out from under "Islam" as a topic, denying it the coherence that could locate its rightful branch on a tree. Now what?

Without definitive answers to the problems of categories and labels, here's what I'll say: calling this project *Magic in Islam* is what allows it to travel through the necessary channels to materialize as a book in the world. Having performed the necessary deconstruction of categories and displayed critical self-awareness, now I'm going to do whatever I want. Maybe this book should just be called *Weird Shit in Islam*. This book is my sandbox to play in, and I have brought some compelling toys. Intersecting with normatively Muslim-looking items such as the Qur'ān or the Prophet, this could all add up to solidify a notion of Muslim magic, or not. At any rate, they're items that popularly go into our considerations of magic, esotericism, and the occult, and I'm interested in these things as engaged by people who call themselves Muslims. So whether or not we can reliably identify anything in the world as "magic" or "Islam," here's a book about magic in Islam.

2

Magic in the Revealed Sources

> The Qur'ān does not necessarily exclude magic from the domain of prophecy.
>
> —CARL ERNST[1]

In the chronicles of a Syrian Jacobite patriarch from the ninth century CE, we find a compelling report of encounter between physical and metaphysical realms. According to the account, villagers on the Euphrates in northern Syria were digging in the soil when they unearthed a stone slab bearing Median inscriptions. Digging under the slab, they then discovered a bronze cauldron that contained a bronze statue with a chain around its neck. Assuming that the statue had been buried by sorcerers, the villagers recruited their own local sorcerers to determine the statue's purpose. The village sorcerers and diviners whispered spells over the statue until it told them, "Sixty thousand demons are imprisoned in this figurine." The demons then asked, "What do you give us? Where shall we go?" The sorcerers then d the chain from the statue's neck and commanded them ossess the monks at Qenneshre. The demons did as they were old, and so the monks began displaying strange behaviors: crowing like roosters, bleating like goats, insulting the saints with disparaging nicknames (Paul was called "Fool Fisherman," for example, and Thomas was dubbed "One Ball"), and throwing themselves into the nearby river and drowning.[2]

This episode is reported to have taken place in the mid-660s, which would place it just three decades after the death of Muḥammad; by this time, Syria would have already come under Muslim rule. Our source, Dionysius of Tel-Mahre, died in 845, which would make him a contemporary of master Muslim traditionists such as Aḥmad ibn Ḥanbal and the scholars whose writings provide our earliest extant sources on Muḥammad's life and mission. Obviously, neither Dionysius nor his Muslim contemporaries were eyewitnesses to the events that they chronicled; their works might tell us about the world of the seventh century, but also reflect their own. They can possibly offer us access to Muḥammad's historical setting, but just as likely provide us with the worldviews of a later era in which people represented that setting in texts.

An introductory look at Islam might reasonably start with its historical origins, and thus begin by painting a picture of the world in which Islam emerged, attempting to set a stage that properly contextualizes the Qur'ān and Muḥammad. Islam can then be understood as a logical product of its time and place, having arrived amid the "monotheistic turn" and gradual decline of polytheism throughout the Mediterranean world, the emergence of "imperial faiths," or theological commitments that fueled the power claims of competing kingdoms, and a proliferation of messianic and apocalyptic sectarian movements led by prophetic or semi-divine figures.

Rooted in the Ḥijāz region of the Arabian Peninsula in the early seventh century CE, Muḥammad's movement crystallized in a sort of liminal zone between superpowers of late antiquity, each with their own official confessional identities. Viewed in this way, his mission becomes a product of intersecting flows between the Christian Byzantines, Zoroastrian Sassanids of what is present-day Iran, and Christian Aksum in what is now Ethiopia. We could locate Islam's arrival on the world scene roughly in the middle of a triangle connecting these three regional powers and consider how their religious currents informed the experience of Muḥammad and what would become the first Muslim community.

While thinking about the world of early Islam, however, we should avoid treating Christianity and Zoroastrianism as abstracted systems that remain more or less consistent across time and place. Religious identities are analogous to racial identities in the sense that their meanings and boundaries are unstable, just as the legal and cultural definitions of "white person" in the United States change dramatically depending on whether we're looking at 1890, 1920, or 1950, with Irish, Greek, Jewish, Arab, and other identities falling in and out of the category. The meanings and defining characteristics of Christianity are also subject to historical change, as one could evidence by a quick glance at the numerous communities, doctrines, and texts that are conceivably "Christian" in one century but pushed out of that category as "heretical" in the next. The point here is that when we read of a Christian empire or Zoroastrian empire, our first reflex might be to refer to Christianity and Zoroastrianism as *we* presently conceptualize them, though these terms do not tell us much about what was happening on the ground in the seventh century CE. We can say that while Islam might have come from a place on the map between kingdoms that named Christian or Zoroastrian confessions as their state ideologies, and which also contained Jewish and other minority populations, we could rather think about the popular practices and beliefs that transgressed the boundaries of these traditions.

This means that we can think of Islam as having originated in a world of magic. Giving attention to magic could provide a chance to consider the encounters, exchanges, and shared modes of knowledge between these imperial faiths. What many would call "magic" (again, said here with extreme caution regarding the separation of magic from religion) crossed religious boundaries. In other words, everyone was doing it. We can look at incantation bowls, love charms, curses, exorcism, astrology, and various methods of divination as technologies known and shared between Jews, Christians, Zoroastrians, and other communities of late antiquity, with or without scripturalist permissions or approval from authoritative institutions. One hint that divination and sorcery were popular among the ancient Israelites is the abundance of biblical verses condemning their practice. Peter Schäfer observes that "the inherent ambivalence of the theoretically forbidden but actually practiced magic"[3] required a theological negotiation with magic's power, in which magic was not expressly denied but rather subsumed within Yahweh's domain.

The popularity of these knowledges and practices across the board suggests that it's not always fruitful to treat religions as dehistoricized, decontextualized clouds of ideas that exist outside the world; if you put an eighth-century Christian, an eighth-century Muslim, and a twenty-first-century Christian or Muslim in a room together, the twenty-first-century believer is probably going to be the odd one out, regardless of his/her faith conviction. "Magical" practices could point to shared assumptions about the nature of the universe and its operations that transcend particular scriptures or churches, such as the power of words and names and the influence of the stars on earthly affairs.

The Qur'ān and Muḥammad

I don't want to fall into a Protestant framework that prioritizes scripture as a religion's organic center and assumes that to understand a religion, you have to first dive into its "Bible"—which implies that if a religion doesn't have its own Bible, it fails to measure up as a "real religion." But for a number of reasons, the Qur'ān is a good place to start. Academic interrogations aside, plenty of Muslims would emphatically affirm the Qur'ān as the most important resource for understanding Islam, and no amount of theoretical agonizing over religion's colonial Protestantization can undo the power of the Qur'ān in Muslim lives. For people who would locate "true" Islam at its origins, the Qur'ān provides the earliest of our sources, dated even by secular scholarship to have emerged in its recognizable form in the decades immediately after Muḥammad—*at the latest*—and plausibly treated as a documentary source from his own lifetime. In comparison, the vast literary corpus devoted to Muḥammad's biography and teachings comes to us much later: his earliest biography, composed well over a century after his death, is only available to us in edited recensions nearly *two* centuries after his death. To examine how magic might have been conceived in seventh-century Mecca, the Qur'ān is our best resource.

In this capacity, however, the Qur'ān can be frustrating. Because the Qur'ān is presented as God's direct speech to Muḥammad, it does not provide the kind of biographical resource on Muḥammad's mission that the Gospels claim for Jesus: God does not speak to Muḥammad for the purpose of telling him his own life story. Rather, as a resource on Muḥammad and the earliest Muslims, the Qur'ān gives us little more than material for educated guessing. Additionally, in contrast to the Bible, the Qur'ān does not present itself as chiefly a source for historical data on the sacred past: we do not find in the Qur'ān the lengthy genealogies or detailed biographies that characterize biblical literature. Rather, the Qur'ān tends to offer sparse, abridged versions of stories, apparently with the assumption that people already have familiarity with the content. The Qur'ān frequently prefaces references to Abraham, Jesus, and other figures with instructions for Muḥammad to remind his people about them. The Qur'ān seems to discuss the stories of biblical prophets not for the purpose of providing new information, but rather in order to draw from common points of reference that could be immediately understood and appreciated by its audience.

Assumption of the audience's prior knowledge means that just as a contemporary news commentator does not have to provide the president's entire biography before offering editorials on a State of the Union address, the Qur'ān leaves out material that is unnecessary to the key point. This presents us with a problem when trying to understand the Qur'ān's references within its broader context of seventh-century Arabia, since the Qur'ān does not tell us much about the specific communities and texts that it engages. Because we are unable to supplement the Qur'ān with sources from its own setting, filling the Qur'ān's gaps makes for a sizable and often impossible challenge.

We could attempt to better understand the Qur'ān through reported sayings of Muḥammad or episodes from his life, as Muslim interpretive traditions suggest. I do not throw these out entirely, but retain critical wariness due to their late arrivals. We can refer to poems from Mecca that might help to paint a picture of the culture in which the Qur'ān emerged, but cannot escape the problem of dating; these pre-Islamic poems are only available to us through *post*-Islamic sources. This does not mean that we abandon all the aforementioned sources, but only that we proceed with mindful caution when making assertions about the Qur'ān's world.

Having been revealed in real time, the Qur'ān often spoke in response to what people were apparently saying to Muḥammad: hence the number of passages that start with, "They say ____________" or "They ask you about ________." From the Qur'ān's representations of its interlocutors, it appears that they had magic on their minds. The three-letter Arabic root associated with sorcery, *s-ḥ-r*, appears sixty-three times in the Qur'ān. (Interestingly, the root can also signify the morning dawn, which accounts for three of those appearances.) In many of these references, we find that the Qur'ān argues to establish itself not only as a supernatural communication, but one of the right kind: a revelation from God, rather than the product of another unseen force. Several of the Qur'ān's mentions of siḥr include defenses against the charge that Muḥammad himself was a practitioner and that the Qur'ān's incomparable eloquence constituted a form of siḥr. According to the Qur'ān's portrayal of Muḥammad's opponents, disbelievers responded to his claims of divine revelation and promise of future resurrection with, "Indeed, this is an obvious sāḥir" (10:2, 11:7). This is also represented as the answer of past disbelievers to the prophets who came to them with clear evidence, such as Jesus (5:110). As the disbelievers in Muḥammad's era had apparently demanded that he perform miracles to prove his claims, the Qur'ān responds that if he did offer them miracles, they would still dismiss him: if God offered the people a written scripture on a page that they could touch with their hands, allowed them to ascend into the heavens themselves, or provided Muḥammad with wondrous treasures and gardens (6:7, 11:7, 26:8), they would still dismiss him as a sāḥir.

In these verses, the charge of siḥr seems to mark the accused as a con artist, a charlatan whose claims of supernatural powers are bolstered by gimmicks. Such is the case in the Qur'ān's story of Moses, which contrasts his genuine miracles against the scams of Pharaoh's sāḥirs. In both the Qur'ān and the Bible, Moses shows that he is not a sāḥir by being a better sāḥir than his opponents. For Schäfer, the biblical treatment of Moses outperforming the Pharaoh's sāḥirs presents the tension between what he observes as magic's theoretical prohibition and continued practice. As this tension is worked out in the battle between Moses and the court sāḥirs, Moses does not deny magic, but shows that true magic belongs to Yahweh.[4]

Moses is far and away the most oft-mentioned prophet in the Qur'ān (referenced by name 136 times, while Muḥammad is mentioned by name only 5 times), and thus is considered a paradigmatic stand-in for Muḥammad. When Moses declares to Pharaoh that he is a messenger from the Lord of all worlds, Pharaoh challenges him to show a sign of his divine mandate. Moses then throws his staff, at which point it transforms into a snake, and withdraws his hand from his cloak, revealing that it has turned bright white. The elites of Pharaoh's court dismiss these feats as tricks from a "learned sāḥir" (*sāḥirun 'alīm*) who wishes to drive Pharaoh from his land. Pharaoh calls for all sāḥirs to be gathered before him. Hoping for a reward from Pharaoh, they challenge Moses to a contest of marvelous feats. The sāḥirs throw their staffs, creating an illusion by which they "bewitched the eyes of the people" (*saḥarū a'yun an-nās*) and terrified them with their great sorcery (*siḥr 'aḍeem*). Here, the *s-ḥ-r* root appears to signify trickery rather than actual supernatural powers. When Moses throws his own staff, which then devours "what they were falsifying" (*mā ya'fikūn*), the sāḥirs recognize the truth of Moses's claims and fall in prostration, declaring their faith in his god (7:104–127). Whether the sāḥirs' tricks were truly made possible by genuine mastery of unseen forces or simply sleight of hand, their fall to Moses establishes siḥr's inferiority to the powers of divinely favored prophets.

The Qur'ān acknowledges that there are multiple ways in which human beings can receive information from the unseen, and thus seeks to distinguish Muḥammad's prophecy as superior to other modes of access. This means defending Muḥammad against association with the *kāhin*, an oracular, priestly, and prophetic figure, commonly marked as "soothsayer" in English translations of the Qur'ān. Throughout the region, kāhins worked as diviners and performed sacrificial rites and guardianship at specific sanctuaries. It would appear that to some of Muḥammad's contemporaries, Muḥammad's claims of supernatural revelations only made him one among numerous kāhins, rather than God's appointed messenger. "So remind," the Qur'ān tells Muḥammad, "for you are not, by the favor of your lord, a kāhin or a madman" (52:29). The term used here for "madman," *majnūn*, signifies a person who has been possessed by a jinn, a being of smokeless fire. Jinns were believed to eavesdrop on celestial assemblies in hope of learning secrets, for which God launched shooting stars at them in punishment (37:6-10). Though Allāh remains lord and master of all the worlds, with nothing transpiring other than what Allāh has permitted, the potential for jinns to breach security and obtain heavenly secrets suggests a system that was created to enable occasional leakages. The porous and permeable barriers between our worldly categories of religion and magic are mirrored by similarly flimsy barriers in the celestial spheres above.

Because soothsayers depended on jinns for privileged information from the heavens, jinns posed a potential threat to divinely guided prophethood as a rival mode of knowledge. The Qur'ān's discussions of jinns, therefore, can be read significantly as a polemic against the role of the kāhin in pre-Islamic society. It might be noteworthy that the Qur'ān does not absolutely deny the possibility of jinns acquiring secrets or transmitting their knowledge to humans. Instead, to put it in the terms of ḥadīth evaluation, knowledge from a jinn comes with a defective *isnād*: neither the jinns nor the soothsayer who communicates with jinns are trustworthy reporters.

While allowing that someone who claims to be privy to the secrets of jinns might be telling the truth, the Qur'ān denounces the jinns as informants. Frequently declaring itself a message to humans and jinns alike, the Qur'ān affirms its supremacy over the jinns upon whom soothsayers rely. However, there are also Muslim jinns: The Qur'ān refers to a gathering of jinns who heard recitation of the Qur'ān and testified to its status as a divine revelation. If the jinns were perceived in pre-Islamic Arabian prophecy as extrahuman, extratheistic sources of secret knowledge, their acts of bearing witness to the Qur'ān could serve as a polemic against their human reporters. The polytheistic prophets or diviners claim jinns as their authorization; Muḥammad claims God as his own; the jinns themselves endorse Muḥammad, thus effectively shutting down the soothsayers and diviners in favor of Muḥammad's movement.

At the start of the seventy-second sūra, popularly titled *al-Jinn*, the jinns are quoted as revealing that they had sought to reach the heavens but found it protected by guards and burning flames, and that they could no longer eavesdrop due to the flames. The jinns then state that they do not know the destined fates of human beings, and that while some jinns are righteous Muslims, others are unjust. Finally, they acknowledge that they can do no harm to God, nor escape him; the unjust from among the jinns will be punished in the hellfire. In this short sequence of verses (72:1–15), the Qur'ān confirms that the jinns are (1) prevented from obtaining celestial secrets, (2) unable to reliably predict the future, (3) powerless against God, (4) potentially liars, and (5) Muslims (at least some of them) who recognize the ultimate truth of the Qur'ān. Rather than represent competition to Muḥammad's prophethood, jinns are portrayed instead as confirming the superiority of the divinely revealed text to whatever they could offer.

The tension between revelation from God and knowledge from spirits resurfaces in the Qur'ān's treatment of Solomon. Standing at our imagined border between religion and other fields such as magic or the occult, Solomon appears as a complex and liminal character, making use of tools on both sides of the binary. Solomon's character in Jewish and Christian literatures had undergone transformation in the centuries prior to Islam, developing from merely a wise king to Hermetic sage, astrologer, magician, exorcist and controller of demons, and even master over the weather. The Qur'ān engages this magical Solomon, portraying him as fluent in the language of birds and commanding jinn soldiers in his army (27:16–17). Solomon is also endowed with command over the wind, though the Qur'ān makes it clear that this power comes through God's favor upon him, rather than Solomon's own capabilities (21:81, 34:12). The Qur'ān, arguing against what were apparently popular ideas about Solomon among its audience, proclaims Solomon's innocence of siḥr. In reference to Israelites who had resorted to siḥr, the Qur'ān states that they "followed what the devils had recited during the reign of Solomon. It was not Solomon who disbelieved, but the devils disbelieved." These devils taught people siḥr and "that which was revealed to the two angels at Babylon, Hārūt and Mārūt." To locate this teaching in Babylon recalls the association of magic with Persian priests from which we get the term "magic." The Qur'ān does not give us much more information about Hārūt and Mārūt; they constitute one of the Qur'ān's gaps that seem to assume prior knowledge. This short reference resonates with the *Book of the Watchers* (I Enoch 1–36), an apocryphal text from the third century BCE that depicts fallen angels ("sons of God") mating with the women of earth and teaching a wealth of previously unknown sciences to humanity, including astrology and sorcery.[5]

Among the secret technologies that Hārūt and Mārūt divulged, the Qur'ān mentions a science "by which they cause separation between a man and his wife." As with its exoneration of Solomon, the Qur'ān clarifies that the two angels were innocent of what they taught; the angels warned their human students with the disclaimer, "We are a trial, so do not disbelieve." In case this knowledge strikes anyone as frightening (or tempting), the Qur'ān asserts that such technologies remain subject to the ruler of all the worlds: "But they do not harm anyone through it except by permission of God." The Qur'ān adds that anyone who indulges in such practices would have no share in the hereafter.

In its brief treatment of siḥr in relation to prophets and angels within this singular verse (2:102), the Qur'ān both condemns siḥr as disbelief and legitimates it as having been revealed to humanity through encounter with angels. Prohibited but not exactly powerless, siḥr is simultaneously dismissed and given a degree of legitimacy.

The Qur'ān offers its own words as a prayer against the harm of siḥr in the 113th sūra, *al-Falāq*. The sūra begins with *Qul*, "Say," presenting God's words to humanity as a prayer that believers can recite back to God:

> Say: I seek refuge with the Lord of the dawn,
> From the evil of what he has created;
> And from the evil of darkness when it spreads,
> And from the evil of the blowers in knots,
> And from the evil of the envious when he envies.

The verses present human beings as vulnerable to the malevolent intentions of others, or at least anxious about the matter. The mention of "blowers in knots" seems to refer to malevolent siḥr or "black magic" practices in the region: ancient Sumerian tablets as well as the Bible discuss sorcery in relation to the tying and loosing of knots, and knot practices remained significant in Jewish folk religion despite biblical condemnation.[6] The final verse resonates with an ancient view of envy not simply as a negative feeling but in fact as a powerful force in the material world. As an assurance against fears of sorcery and ill will, the sūra comforts its reader with the promise of Allāh's shelter. Moreover, with its command to recite these words, the sūra itself becomes a shelter, a divinely revealed counter-incantation against spells and the evil eye.

Possible ambiguities in the second verse, "From the evil of what he has created," allow for multiple readings. There could be more than one way to think about the "he." Qur'ān translators often follow Victorian English literary conventions and capitalize the divine pronoun, presenting the verse as "from the evil of what He has created"; in this case, the sūra clearly articulates that God gives you refuge from the evil that God has created, which could include anything from the malevolent acts of humans and demons to the natural danger of snakes and scorpions. Since God created everything, it isn't necessarily a theological provocation to call God the creator of evil; but because Arabic does not have capital letters, this modern "He" isn't something that we can find in the original text. In other words, we don't know that the verse describes evil that God created; though God is technically the only one who creates, the verse could refer to the work of another person, a specific evil at a specific moment from which Muḥammad needed refuge.

This provides one of those moments at which the Qur'ān is frequently read in conversation with the details of Muḥammad's life and the original Muslims, as represented in the corpus of prophetic biographies and ḥadīth traditions. The accounts of Muḥammad's actions and teachings provide a supplementary compendium through which the Qur'ān can be understood and ambiguous verses might be clarified. As opposed to the fixed limits of the Qur'ān, the biographical material concerning Muḥammad is vast and seemingly endless, though the corpus has variously constricted or expanded depending on Muslim scholars' methods of evaluating materials' authenticity. Within this corpus, we encounter elaborations on the Qur'ān's treatment of siḥr: the Qur'ān condemns siḥr without prescribing a penalty, for example, while prophetic reports sentence the practitioner of siḥr to death.

Early Muslim exegetes understood *al-Falāq* as a response to a particular episode in Muḥammad's prophetic mission. A special category of biographical reports concerning Muḥammad, known as *asbāb al-nazūl*, or "occasions of revelation," connects specific sūras and verses in the Qur'ān to the circumstances in which they descended upon Muḥammad. As the Qur'ān was revealed in bits and pieces to Muḥammad over a twenty-three-year period, divine communications often made direct reference to happenings in the community: questions that were asked of Muḥammad by followers or opponents, theological debates with other communities, or incidents in which Allāh would reveal new verses to elaborate on an earlier point, bring clarity to what had been vague, address issues ranging from recent battles to marital relations, or even correct Muḥammad's errors. In the case of *al-Falāq*'s anti-siḥr polemic, asbab al-nazūl traditions present the sūra as having been revealed after Muḥammad himself had fallen victim to magical harm.

An account of Muḥammad temporarily succumbing to the powers of siḥr, attributed to his wife 'Ā'isha, remains in the most trusted of the canonical Sunnī ḥadīth collections. 'Ā'isha tells us that Muḥammad had been afflicted with a kind of siḥr that made him believe that he had engaged in sex with his wives when he had not. Muḥammad later told 'Ā'isha that Allāh intervened on his behalf, sending two men (angels?) to him. As Muḥammad was lying on the floor, the men sat at opposite ends of Muḥammad's body, one near his head and the other at his feet.

"What is wrong with this man?" asked the man seated by Muḥammad's head. His partner answered that Muḥammad had been afflicted with siḥr. The first man then asked who was responsible; the second told him that it was a Jewish sāḥir from the tribe of Banu Zurayq, Labīd ibn al-'Aṣam. The inquirer then asked about the materials that Labīd used for his project. The man at Muḥammad's feet answered that Labīd had obtained Muḥammad's comb and used hairs from it. In their final exchange, he explained that the comb and hairs were in a skin of pollen from a male date palm tree, which Labīd had placed in a well; the man named the well and said that the items were under a stone. Muḥammad then headed for the well and removed Labīd's siḥr kit. In his account to 'Ā'isha, Muḥammad added that the water looked like the infusion of henna, and the nearby date-palm trees looked like the heads of devils. This narration, coming to us through various chains of reporters, appears in the most authoritative Sunnī collections of ḥadīths, the Kutub al-Sitta (literally "Six Books"), in association with various topics; the great Bukhārī, whose ḥadīth collection is widely considered the most prestigious of these six, includes it in his chapter on medicine. Another version describes the sorcerer as using not Muḥammad's comb or hairs to perform his siḥr, but rather a knotted rope that he had hidden in a well. In this version, the angel Gabriel informs Muḥammad what had happened, and Muḥammad retrieves the rope and breaks Labīd's siḥr by untying the knots. In still another version, the attack is attributed not to Labīd, but three or four of his daughters, who tied knots against the Prophet.[7] This would resonate with *Al-Falāq*'s gendered mention of "blowers in knots," feminizing the label to target specifically women who engage in the practice. Labīd's daughters placed their knots in the spathe of a male palm tree, which could have held resonance with the target being Muḥammad's sexuality: in male palm trees, the spathe houses a substance that becomes white and emits an odor comparable to semen.[8]

Interpretive traditions associate Muḥammad's rescue from Labīd's siḥr with the revelation of *al-Falāq* and also the Qur'ān's final sūra, *an-Nās*, which also begins with a divine command to speak and assures the reciter of protection against sinister forces:

> Say: I seek refuge with the Lord of humanity,
> The King (or Owner) of humanity,
> The god of humanity,
> From the evil of the whisperer
> Who whispers in the chests of humanity,
> From among the jinns and humanity.

In the version that charges Labīd's daughters with the attack, the knots are numbered at eleven, which happens to be the combined number of verses between the two sūras; it is said that with each verse that Muḥammad recited, one of the knots became untied and thus lost its power.[9]

These two sūras, known together as the Mu'awwidhitayn for their shared references to seeking refuge (*'awadha*), attained tremendous significance for the early Muslim community, reportedly even during Muḥammad's lifetime. The sūras are widely regarded as powerful tools for *ruqya*, the prophetic technology that operates as a protection and antidote against malevolent siḥr's effects. Muḥammad is quoted as praising the Mu'awwidhitayn as the best two sūras ever recited and even using them as treatment for ailments such as scorpion bites. Traditions describe Muḥammad practicing a nightly ritual in which he recited these sūras (along with a third, *al-Ikhlas*) while breathing into his palms, then rubbed his hands over his body—essentially covering himself with the recitation of these protective verses. 'Ā'isha is also portrayed as performing this practice for Muḥammad during his final illness, which would point to God's absolute power over all modes of ruqya and siḥr, since Muḥammad ultimately did not survive.

Some sources report controversy among the earliest Muslims as to whether the two Mu'awwidhitayn belonged within the bounds of the Qur'ān or comprised a prayer outside the text. Before the full codification of the Qur'ān in the early decades after the Prophet's death, Muḥammad's Companion Ibn Mas'ūd is reported to have excluded them from his own Qur'ān codex. Nonetheless, the Mu'awwidhitayn would find not only inclusion within the "official" text of the Qur'ān, but added support from the numerous traditions regarding their special prestige. Controversy over the sūras' placement in the Qur'ān could relate to these numerous reports of Muḥammad praising their virtues: Reports on behalf of the Mu'awwidhitayn could suggest that at one time, the sūras' advocates had to argue for their place in the scripture. On the other hand, the question would have been one of genre: while these Mu'awwidhitayn were understood to have been divinely revealed, perhaps their stylistic departure of starting with God's command "Say," might have provoked confusion over whether they were sūras. Ibn Mas'ūd's codex was reported to have also excluded *al-Fātiḥa*, which reads not as God's statement to human beings but as a human prayer to God.

The Mu'awwidhitayn encourage reconsideration of the line

that we assume to exist naturally between magic and religion. For their placement in the Qur'ān, we would categorize the Mu'awwidhitayn as items of *religious* scripture; but the sūras offer more than what many expect scriptures to provide. The verses do not only communicate a message about God as protector, but actually act as protections against siḥr through their aural or visual reproduction. Some scholars, struggling with the problem of defining magic, lean toward a functionalist approach: this approach allows that maybe magic lacks an essential nature and defining characteristics that set it apart from religion, but asserts that we can identify magic by looking at the effects that practitioners desire from its use. When viewed through a functionalist lens, the same piece of scripture can alternately fall into religious or magical categories depending on a believer's specific interest in it. Muslims can read these sūras as divine communications and perform high-level analysis of their content and form, or treat the words themselves as full of power when we recite or wear them in the original Arabic—with or without comprehension. The Mu'awwidhitayn point to the real power of the Qur'ān as not only a thesis, but a divine energy field. It is in part for this that Carl Ernst considers the Qur'ān to be not so much the "Muslim Bible," but closer to being the Muslim Christ: the recitation of the Qur'ān provides an access and encounter comparable to the Eucharist's assimilation of Christ's blood and body into the body of the believer.[10]

The Qur'ān condemns those who breathe onto knots and offers itself as refuge from their violence. Muḥammad exhales the Mu'awwadhitayn's verses into his open hands and rubs the verses' energies over his body. In the ḥadīth corpus, Muḥammad even designates the blowing of knots for siḥr as *shirk*, attaching the practice to idolatry. This can make for complications; if knot-blowing constitutes idol worship, yet afflicts human beings as a real force that they cannot fend off by themselves, then the sciences of idolatry are in fact given some credit. It is not exactly that they are powerless, but only less powerful than Allāh. The means by which believers can protect themselves from magicians look more than a little like the magicians' own tactics. Bukhārī and other ḥadīth scholars telling us that Muḥammad recommended eating seven 'ajwa dates every morning for immunity against siḥr sounds kind of like magic itself; for Bukhārī, this prophetic precaution was not magic but medicine.

Can we draw a line between religion and magic on the basis that the sūras' seeking refuge in God preserves God as the holder of power, as opposed to spells that *command* spirits to serve human practitioners? Or do we think of reciting the Mu'awwadhitayn as religion, rather than magic, simply because it takes place in a theistic setting, and we conflate authentic religion with theism? If the Prayer of Mary, a Coptic Christian text that asks for Mary to employ her protective powers on behalf of its reciter, switched out Mary's name for another spiritual entity, would the text change from a prayer to an incantation?[11] If you repeat the correct prescription of words, Mary or Allāh can repel demons from your presence and deflect the negative energies of human beings who wish for harm upon you. But what makes this a prayer and not a spell?

So for readers of the Qur'ān, where could dīn end and siḥr begin, or could there be types of siḥr that achieve legitimacy within dīn? We find premodern Muslim intellectuals constructing this binary on their own terms. In his *Fihrist*, written sometime around the turn of the eleventh century CE, Ibn al-Nadīm identifies the unacceptable *saḥara* (practitioners of siḥr) not by their ability to recruit demons and jinns to serve them, but only by the method by which they attain this power. Unacceptable saḥara were the ones who attracted these unseen creatures by giving them offerings and engaging in the behaviors that gave them joy—namely, illegal or blasphemous acts that offended God. At the same time, Ibn al-Nadīm acknowledged that some practitioners could achieve the same influence over demons and jinns through devotional acts, constant prayer, and obedience to sacred law. These saḥara did not subdue spirits by their own means, and did not betray the commandments of God to obtain this power, but were granted the privilege of controlling them by God. Among these pious and sharī'a-compliant saḥara, Ibn al-Nadīm mentions an Ibn Hilāl, who was "served and spoken to [by jinns], and was known for wonderful deeds and actions of goodness, as well as for seals of tested value."[12]

Both illicit and licit siḥr became known to humans through acts of supernatural pedagogy. In contrast to illicit siḥr, the origins of which would be traced in some sources to the Devil's granddaughter, Baydakh, licit siḥr was a divine revelation taught by its first practitioner, the prophet Solomon.[13] Ibn al-Nadīm justified his division of licit and illicit siḥr through an understanding of the Qur'ān itself, which describes power over jinns as a privilege granted to a prophet, who certainly would not have been called a sāḥir. Depicting a prophet who does sorcererish things, the Qur'ān's representation of Solomon opens a space for siḥr, while subjecting siḥr's power to a certain pious regulation, staying cognizant that God remains in charge. Solomon's prophetic station seems to make his particular siḥr okay. More often, attaching siḥr's stigma to religious thinkers serves to delegitimize their projects. Premodern Muslim scholars opposed to Mu'tāzilī thought produced a genealogy to discredit them as heirs to siḥr: Mu'tāzilī thinkers were alleged to have learned their doctrine of the Qur'ān's createdness from executed arch-heretic Jahm ibn Ṣafwān, who learned it from Ja'd ibn Adham, who learned it from Abān ibn Sam'ān, who learned it from Ṭalūb, the first to promulgate the doctrine in writing; and Ṭalūb had learned it from his uncle, Labīd ibn al-'Aṣam, the bewitcher of the Prophet.[14] Rationalist theology in a sāḥir's hands becomes another magical weapon, a tool to create mischief and division, while critics could link excessive theological speculation and illicit siḥr as sharing in a denial of God's power.

Given the complexities of interpreting texts, locating the line of differentiation between a prophet's religion and a magician's sorcery seems to be lacking in usefulness, as Solomon simultaneously upholds and subverts the boundary. It might have less to do with the actions performed or even the underlying logic of the actions, but rather the question of why the actions and their logic are able to work. Is this actually religion vs. something other than religion, or good religion vs. bad religion? Belief in the power of special speech-acts to achieve material change seems to cross the line from religion into magic only when someone decides that your religion is wrong.

Deconstructing Siḥr

Of course, attempting to discuss "what the Qur'ān says" about anything confronts the problem of textual meaning. A text's meaning does not only come from the author (even a divine Author) upon a passive reader, but also emerges as the reader processes these words through her own world, experience, and knowledge. The Qur'ān's ultimate claims on magic, therefore, emerge as a product of conversation between the scripture and its believers. The Qur'ān presents itself as an answer to the threats of siḥr and assorted technologies of secrets and harm, but the real significance of the Qur'ān's anti-siḥr polemic can change between readers. Certainly, the Qur'ān's original audience included people who believed in siḥr and the evil eye as actual forces that could pose serious threats to their welfare. The Qur'ān makes an argument for them to trust in Allāh against these evil powers, and could even be interpreted as offering itself not only as anti-siḥr discourse, but as an actual artifact of anti-siḥr technology, a prayer that will shut down the efforts of sorcerers, knot-blowers, and the envious. The Qur'ān's condemnation of siḥr, however, remains sufficiently open that it can produce different meanings. In the late nineteenth century and throughout the twentieth century, as many Muslim intellectuals approached their scriptures through a particular lens of scientific rationality and valorization of "modern values," the Qur'ān's treatment of siḥr was read in ways that did not assume siḥr to be real. Important figures from a variety of points in modern Muslim thought, from Muslim Brotherhood ideologues to Ahmadiyya missionaries to liberal and progressive Muslim reformists, have read the Qur'ān's anti-siḥr statements with a lens of modern skepticism. The Qur'ān still condemns siḥr, but siḥr's exact threat is often less that of satanically empowered violence than a regression into backward thinking, more superstition than sin. To many, the question of magic's reality relates to that of the Devil's reality, that is, whether the Devil/Shayṭān is literally a personified being who actively interferes in human events or rather an allegorical representation of human selfishness.

For those who read *al-Falāq* and other passages through this perspective, the Qur'ān speaks with a rationalist voice that endeavors to liberate the mind from superstition. Even the Qur'ān commentary of Islamist thinker Sayyid Quṭb, whom many would superficially dismiss as a "fundamentalist," describes siḥr as primarily an act of psychological warfare, by which someone uses illusions and head games to influence others. In his commentary on *al-Falāq*, Quṭb briefly mentions the bewitching of Muḥammad by Labīd ibn 'Aṣam, gently dismissing the story as coming from "a few unsupported narratives, some of which have been quoted by authentic sources."[15] Through these readings, the Qur'ān becomes a call for rationalist enlightenment (within limits) against what its interpreters deride as primitive ignorance; this is why Muḥammad, when challenged to perform miracles as Moses had, offered only divinely revealed discourse.

It would be wrong to present a simple binary in which premodern Muslims read the Qur'ān in a particular way because they really believed in magic, while modern Muslims read the Qur'ān as making a rationalist argument against magic. Obviously, our modern world is filled with people of all religions and no religion who believe in the reality of what we call magic, sorcery, witchcraft, or siḥr. Some would be surprised, however, by the degree of *pre*modern Muslim skepticism regarding magic. In Islam's early centuries, thinkers from multiple theological and legal schools rejected sorcery as mere deception. The Hanafī jurist Abū Bakr al-Jaṣṣāṣ, who died less than four centuries after Muḥammad, argued that the falsehood of siḥr is proven by the poverty and marginalization of its practitioners; if sorcerers possessed real power, they would be appropriating the riches of kings and ruling the world, rather than attempting to hustle common people in the marketplace.[16] Though the chains of transmission were strong enough for seminal ḥadīth scholars such as Bukhārī to include Muḥammad's bewitching in their collections, empowering the story with full canonical gravitas, some Muslim thinkers rejected the episode as inauthentic on theological grounds. For these interpreters, Allāh would not have allowed sorcerers to enjoy even a temporary abuse and degradation of Muḥammad, having promised in the Qur'ān both that he would protect Muḥammad and that sorcerers were doomed to failure.[17]

When modern Muslim rationalists read the Qur'ān's discussions of magic as condemnations of irrational superstition, rather than as an assurance of safety against very real demonic powers, we cannot simply reduce this reading to a by-product of modernity. The tradition is vast enough to offer premodern resources for a variety of modern projects. If anything, we could consider the degree to which intellectuals prior to modern printing wrote mainly for each other's eyes, rather than the uneducated masses, while the media technologies and mass education of today's world could enable premodern thinkers' works to travel much wider than they ever would have imagined or even desired. At any rate, while we can examine shifting modes of knowledge and changing historical trends, Arnold Yasin Mol points out that "the rejection of supernatural sorcery is not simply a modern position formed under the influence of the modern scientific worldview."[18] Another way to say it, with an eye for the anticolonial consequences: Muslims did not need European invaders to teach them about empirical rationality.

Another important point to consider in regard to the Qur'ān's capacity for multiple meanings: just as the meanings of the Qur'ān's opposition to siḥr could read in different ways, depending on whether one believed in siḥr as a literal force or ridiculed belief in siḥr as superstition, we can also find complexity regarding the precise definition of what the Qur'ān has condemned. Before fulfilling a scriptural command, readers of the scripture must decide for themselves what a specific term signifies. For example, Muslims might agree that the Qur'ān prohibits intoxication, but disagree on intoxication's boundaries as a category. This is exactly what happened as believers encountered unfamiliar new substances, such as coffee and cannabis, that clearly impacted their consumers' personalities; did the effects place these substances in the same prohibited class as wine? Muslims even argued over whether all alcoholic beverages were forbidden; were intoxicating beverages made from dates in a different category than wine made from grapes? Similarly, siḥr is a social construction. Scripturalist believers can speak with confidence that Allāh prohibits siḥr and that Muḥammad had named siḥr as one of seven particularly offensive transgressions, but they still must figure out for themselves what actually counts within the limits of the term. While early jurists generally regarded siḥr as idolatrous, constitutive of apostasy, and a cause of harm, there were also jurists who distinguished between siḥr intended to injure others and siḥr used in healing. The latter, ruqya, wields foundational authority in the personal practice of Muḥammad. Sa'īd ibn al-Musayyab, recognized as one of the "seven jurists of Medina," allowed what could have been regarded as siḥr if performed for healing, the Ḥanafī school made a legal distinction between protective and active siḥr, and Ibn Ḥanbal refrained from condemning healers to the same class as sāḥirs.[19] For these scholars, the chief concern in conceptualizing siḥr was not the technology itself, but its intended purpose.

It is for this reason that saying simply, "The Qur'ān forbids magic," whether right or wrong, doesn't really tell us much. Throughout Islam's history, Muslims have been engaging in sciences and practices that other Muslims would revile as unacceptable innovations or even demonic arts, but these controversies cannot be reduced to Muslims either "following the Qur'ān" or abandoning its commands. Rather than ask what the Qur'ān tells us about magic, it would be more fruitful to examine ways in which believers in the Qur'ān locate their own values and knowledges within its revealed text, or even the ways in which God's speech functions as more than text, as something beyond textuality.

3

The Force of the Letters

A book of magic is also a magical book. It not only tells how to perform magical works, but shares in the numinous qualities and powers of the rites it contains.

—RICHARD KIECKHEFER[1]

Books can be magical without actually containing magic.

—OWEN DAVIES[2]

Kieckhefer's observation refers to the "book of magic" in its most straightforward and plain-sense meaning: the literary genre of the grimoire, compendium of charms, spell-casting formulas and recipes, and instructions for producing efficacious talismans. This is a genre to which Muslim scholars have contributed, most notably in the examples of al-Būnī's *Shams al-Ma'ārif* (*Sun of Knowledge*) and the *Ghāyat al-Ḥakīm* (*The Aim of the Sage*), unreliably attributed to mathematician al-Majrīṭī. The

Ghāyat in particular achieved some fame in European occultism upon its thirteenth-century translation into Spanish and then Latin upon the orders of Castile's Christian ruler Alfonso the Wise, and subsequent circulation as the *Picatrix*.[3]

What interests me about the magic powers of books, however, is not the content of the grimoire, but the observation cited above that books can wield "magical" powers without actually being about "magic." Can an *anti*-magical book also be magical? Most readers would agree that in its plain-sense meaning, the Qur'ān presents itself in opposition to magic: the Qur'ān explicitly denies its critics' charges that its verses are only siḥr, and positions itself against malevolent siḥr of dark arts and the trickery of Pharaoh's court wizards. But could the Qur'ān operate as a kind of grimoire in its own right? The Qur'ān gives people instructions for dealing with beneficent energies of the unseen realm. Perhaps more importantly, if a book that does not contain magic might still be magical, the Qur'ān itself becomes a primary instrument for such interactions.

In popular treatments, the Qur'ān is conceptualized as a conduit through which these beneficent energies can flow and reach humans. The energies could be described with the Arabic term *baraka*, which is generally translated as "blessings" but could perhaps more accurately be described as something like the Force. The Qur'ān tells believers how to attain baraka, but also operates as a resource in which baraka can be located and accessed. The Qur'ān commands prayer, is recited in prayer, and functions independently of formal prayer as an act of devotion by its mere presence, whether aural or material. The Qur'ān can be thought of as a magical book to the extent that it shares in the divine power of which it speaks.

The Qur'ān's full relationship to magic, therefore, goes far beyond what we consider the text to be arguing in its prescriptions and condemnations. Whatever we might hear the Qur'ān telling us about Allāh's judgments on magic, the Qur'ān operates as more than a set of theses and legal commands: it also exists in the world as an artifact, a trace of divine presence endowed with what Travis Zadeh calls "miraculous charisma."[4] When discussing the Qur'ān, we often fall into the trap of treating the Qur'ān exclusively as a book, focusing on questions of its authorship, content, and interpretation while forgetting the Qur'ān's life beyond its discourse. For many non-Muslims who seek an introductory glimpse of Islam, the first impulse is to pick up a mass-printed copy of the Qur'ān and read it, often in translation, purely as a source of doctrinal statements. This was how I first attempted to learn about Islam, having come from a Christian background with a particular set of assumptions about scripture. Such an approach excludes so much of what the Qur'ān actually does in lived Muslim experience.

More than simply an archive of statements and meanings demanding comprehension and intellectual study, the Qur'ān is widely regarded as a point of access to transcendent forces and an abundance of beneficent energies, which can potentially be harnessed through relations to its words. The words matter, but they are capable of mattering as things other than words. What would it mean to reproduce God's exact speech with your own body, recite particular verses to achieve specific results, and prioritize correct pronunciation of the sounds over analysis of the message? The words *mean* things, but they also *do.*

The revelation, or *nazul* (literally "descending"), of the Qur'ān's words is reported in the canonical ḥadīth corpus as having produced observable physical effects on Muḥammad, such as excessive perspiration and a dramatic increase in his body weight. Considering Muḥammad's body as the material point of mediation between metaphysical and physical worlds, the channel through which Allāh's speech entered the world, it would seem natural that the Companions regarded Muḥammad's Qur'ān-manifesting body as a locus of baraka. They collected his sweat in jars, drank water from his ritual ablutions, and reported numerous miracles involving his saliva. Pious heroes of the early generations, such as the Companion Anas ibn Mālik, caliph Mu'āwiya, and ḥadīth scholar Ibn Ḥanbal, even arranged to be buried with relics from his body, such as his hairs or fingernail clippings.

The Qur'ān flowed through Muḥammad's body as a material force. What would it mean to have that energy hanging from your necklace?

Allāh's revelation of the 113th and 114th sūras to Muḥammad as a protective prayer against the attacks of sorcerers, and Muḥammad's reported use of these sūras in what could be called magical or counter-magical measures, opens a space to think of the Qur'ān not only in terms of what it says about magic, but what it *does* in relation to magic, whether as defense against magic or as its own category of licit "white magic." The Qur'ān features prominently in a number of practices that could be called more or less nondiscursive, in which the presence of the Qur'ān sometimes counts more than its meanings.

Foremost among the Qur'ān's sūras for healing and protective practices is its opening sūra, *al-Fātiḥa*, which would seem intuitive due to this sūra's role in formal Muslim ritual. For its repeated recitations in the five daily prayers—seventeen times if a Muslim only does the obligatory prayers, but a total of thirty-three times if s/he also performs supplementary Sunna prayers—and not even including its recitation in other prayers, *al-Fātiḥa* makes a strong case for being the single most repeated devotional text in human history. *Al-Fātiḥa* also holds a unique appeal for its speaking from the perspective of humans addressing God, rather than the usual opposite (apart from portions in the Qur'ān prefaced by God's command, "Say"). In the ḥadīth corpus, traditions can be found in which Muḥammad's Companions use recitations of *al-Fātiḥa* to heal suffering people from ailments such as scorpion stings, snake bites, and madness. Narrations of *al-Fātiḥa*'s special healing properties and the example of Muḥammad reciting the 113th and 114th sūras into his hands and rubbing their power over his body present the Qur'ān as a technology of protection, capable of functioning in ways other than simply as a text to be read and understood. Through the exhalation of God's speech into his hands, the Prophet is able to redirect the flows of baraka upon himself through embodied contact.

In "popular" or "folk" practices across a variety of historical settings, sometimes within or beyond the approval of formal religious authorities, Muslims have made use of the Qur'ān as a way of accessing and attracting these energies for themselves and their loved ones. For reasons articulated above, prime selections include *al-Fātiḥa*, *al-Falāq*, and *al-Nās*. Other sūras and short passages also find usage, based either on the Prophet's habitual uses of them or on interpretations of their relevance to the matter of healing, such as 17:82 ("And we sent down in the Qur'ān that which is a healing and a mercy to those who believe: to the unjust it causes nothing but loss after loss"). Premodern saints, scholars, and sorcerers alike expressed confidence in the writing of Qur'ān verses for protective and medicinal amulets. No less a scholarly giant than the ninth-century traditionist Aḥmad ibn Ḥanbal, according to his son, personally wrote Qur'ān-based amulets as a treatment for afflictions ranging from fear to a woman having difficulty in delivering her child.[5]

The passage 17:82 is included among five "verses of healing" (along with 9:15, 10:57, 16:69, 26:80, and 41:44) that each mentioned some form of the *sh-f-'* root, which carries connotations of healing. The letters themselves functioned as vessels of divine power, even when broken down and losing their function as discourse. Al-Shiblī wrote the letter ق into the hand of a man afflicted with jinn possession, drew seven circles around it, and ordered the man to lick it, which successfully drove out the jinn. In her discussion of the episode, Amira El-Zein refers to the various names of God that start with the letter, considering their possible relationships to the letter's healing property: Al-Qādir (the Powerful), al-Qahhar (the Conqueror), al-Qawī (the Mighty), al-Qayyūm (the Everlasting); the letter also signifies the *qalb* (heart) and obviously the Qur'ān itself. "All of these words," she explains, "bear an undeniable symbolic meaning";[6] the question, however, would be whether the letter functions as a symbolic reference to divine names and other items—in which case the letter acts as a prayer, an act of language—or actually carries and transmits powers associated with those terms with material force. This question, for those concerned with its theological implications, would determine the difference between devotional prayer and magical spell.

Beyond healing, verses that discuss other themes could provide support for related needs: Another series of five verses or verse-pairs (2:246, 3:181, 4:76-77, 5:31, 13:78-79) has been observed on talismans made for support in warfare. These five citations include fifty appearances of the letter ق, which in this case would become relevant for its location in the *q-t-l* root that expresses meanings of fighting or killing.[7] In addition to the use of relevant verses for specific causes, the entire material copy (*muṣḥaf*) of the Qur'ān can bring baraka, even if in a miniature reproduction that's too small to actually read, but can hang from a car's rearview mirror. The Qur'ān does not need to be legible or comprehensible in order to perform.

Some healing practices involve the drinking of water affected by encounter with the Qur'ān: a Muslim could pour water into a vessel bearing the Qur'ānic script, or write verses and then dissolve the ink into water, in which the person in need of healing literally ingests the Qur'ān.[8] Early pious scholars such as Ḥasan al-Baṣrī allowed for the ill to drink water that had been used to wash textual reproductions of the Qur'ān on wood or other materials; al-Baghawī endorsed the writing of Qur'ān verses on sweets or food for the sick to eat.[9] Ja'far al-Ṣādiq, sixth of the twelve Imāms in Ithna Ash'arī ("Twelver") Shī'ī tradition, is reported as a source for Qur'ān-based medicine. In one of the prescriptions attributed to him, *al-Fātiḥa* is written along with the 112th, 113th, and 114th sūras and a special prayer, all of which are swallowed on an empty stomach and washed down with rainwater as a cure for colic.[10]

Though a general belief in the healing and protective powers of the Qur'ān claims precedent in Muḥammad's own practices, as reported in the most widely accepted sources on his life and teachings, there remains an occasional tension in regard to these practices. As Ingrid Mattson observes, these acts of drinking Qur'ān-infused water or wearing verses as necklaces would concern "some imams and scholars, who see in them the risk of ascribing healing power to water, paper, and pendants rather than to God."[11] As in the case of astrology and other practices, at stake is God's absolute control over all things. Some uses of the Qur'ān in healing or protection would be condemned by scholars in modern Sunnī revivalist movements as constituting idolatry. However, Mattson explains, the counter-argument affirms practitioners' devotion and surrender to God, as they perceive their practices as a "logical extension of the belief that the Qur'ān, as the eternal Word of God, occupies a status different from any created thing."[12] The potential access to power lies not in the ink or water, but in the eternal, uncreated speech of the lord of all worlds.

The Qur'ān as an Anti-Demon System

In her ethnographic study of healers and "demon specialists" in Cairo, Gerda Sengers observes popular narratives about sorcerers performing a kind of metaphysical judo with the Qur'ān, seemingly redirecting its flows of beneficent energies to do harm. Directed by a jinn or shayṭān, the sorcerer writes the verses of *al-Fātiḥa* in reverse order, using menstrual blood or blood from sacrificed birds as ink, puts torn pages of the Qur'ān in his sandals, wears them in the toilet, touches the Qur'ān after washing his genitals with milk, and writes amulets using his semen.[13] Reports of these practices come from the shaykhs and imāms who provide cures and protections against them, rather than actual sorcerers, and could be considered urban legends. At any rate, though it seems reasonable that such malevolent practitioners would be considered unbelievers for their treatment of the divine text, they still operate firmly within a Muslim cosmology: their acts of blasphemy preserve an ironic investment in the things that they desecrate. They remain "Muslim" in a sense, just as some contemporary Satanists would not self-identify as Christian but nonetheless construct an opposition to Christianity from *within* its traditions and sacred sources, still working in accordance with what they understand to be Christian logics. If these sorcerers are fictional characters, stories of their deriving demonic power from Qur'ān desecration reveal something about how these forces are imagined to flow.

The Qur'ān makes references to the Devil (*al-Shayṭān*) as an avowed enemy of humanity, demons (*shayṭān*, pl. *shayaṭīn*) who act as his agents, and jinns, who are made of smokeless fire. The relationship between these beings is not entirely clear from the Qur'ānic text alone; demons and jinns are often conflated as one species, and the Devil tends to be identified in popular understanding as a jinn, rather than a fallen angel.[14] Common narratives usually portray jinns as evil or mischievous, but they can also appear to be as morally complex as human beings. Muslim scholars have taken their existence seriously, even considering the legal question of whether jinns and humans could intermarry; Mālik, foundational figure for the Mālikī legal school, argued that such a marriage was not itself a violation of sacred law, but added that it seemed undesirable.[15] One ḥadīth scholar in the eighteenth century presented a narration whose chain of transmission included two jinn reporters.[16] Belief in these creatures, though subject to a variety of interpretations, by no means violates established norms or constructions of "orthodoxy."

It is also widely recognized that jinns can possess humans, causing them to appear deranged or engage in impious behaviors, and requiring exorcism by a trained specialist. The Prophet performed exorcisms, setting a precedent that would be followed by great traditionists such as Ibn Ḥanbal.[17] Throughout what is called the "Muslim World," from Morocco to the Sudan to Saudi Arabia to Pakistan to Indonesia, we find diverse traditions of human bodies coming under possession or occupation by jinns. It is beyond our scope here to track every local variant of jinn possession, but we can at least observe that across Muslim exorcism traditions, the Qur'ān frequently appears as a chief weapon. The Qur'ān offers not only a source of authentic information about jinns, but also a functionally reliable protection against them. The Qur'ān's anti-jinn power can be magnified by modern technology, as playing recorded Qur'ān recitations can produce an atmosphere unattractive for jinns.[18] From her ethnographic work in Cairo, Gerda Sengers reports *al-Fātiḥa*, *al-Falāq* and *al-Nās* in tandem, and verse 2:255, the "Verse of the Throne" (*Ayat al-Kursī*) to be efficacious in jinn defense and expulsion, with readings of the ninety-ninth sūra and the first ten verses of the thirty-seventh sūra in accelerated cases.[19] Though jinns are diverse in their religious affiliations, and some are even Muslims who bear witness to the Qur'ān's truth, recitation of the Qur'ān can repel malicious jinns.

Through all of this transdiscursive materiality and performativity, however, the message still matters. While employments of the Qur'ān in compelling and repelling jinns call attention to its power as a material artifact (in written amulets and digested ink) and the capacity of its vocalization to act with force upon the unseen, Qur'ān-based exorcism also relies on the Qur'ān's function as divine speech. Because the Qur'ān addresses its commands to both jinns and humans alike, the Qur'ān's verses can be cited in persuasive arguments that jinns must respect. Barbara Drieskens reports from her fieldwork in Cairo the story of a shaykh who exorcised a jinn from a young girl through a rational argument in which he referred to Qur'ānic verses that convinced the jinn to leave.[20]

Gods of Text

In the early centuries of Islam, a number of major developments affected the Qur'ān's potential and significance as a resource for what could be called magic. First was the codification of the Qur'ān as a fixed, stable text, traditionally seen as having been achieved in the caliphate of 'Uthmān and later finalized in elaborations upon the Arabic script, which established the Qur'ān as a coherent object with a reliable form. Second, the Qur'ān's world was radically changed by the rising importance of writing and paper in a historical setting that had been characterized chiefly by oral tradition. This meant that the Qur'ān (whose very name, meaning "The Recitation," suggests an emphasis on aurality) would find increasing materialization in written form, leading to new applications as protective or healing amulets and talismans—and also new legal questions, as scholars considered whether such uses were appropriate.[21] Third, after bitterly divisive theological controversies that culminated in state crackdowns of dissenting scholars, Muslim thinkers established belief in the Qur'ān's uncreated nature—that is, the Qur'ān's status as having always existed beyond time and space, rather than having been created at a particular moment—as essential to their construction of Sunnī identity. Belief in the Qur'ān's uncreatedness brought an additional consequence: belief in its building blocks, Arabic words and the letters that combine to form them, as transcending normal human language. For mystically inclined thinkers, therefore, Arabic letters could be imagined as cosmic principles in their own right. This helps to understand the mystical visions of Ibn al-'Arabī, who witnessed Allāh as the two letters that spelled *Hū* ("He"), *ha* and *waw*, on a red carpet. In another vision, Ibn al-'Arabī ascended into the heavens and experienced sexual intercourse with all of the letters of the alphabet. When the Qur'ān is imagined as standing beyond time and space, the Arabic alphabet becomes more than mere letters; rather, the alphabet appears as a set of cosmic principles in its own right, a resource for understanding the structures of the created universe and the processes by which the Creator operated. Mughīra ibn Sa'īd (d. 736), an accused sorcerer described by Marshall Hodgson as the "first Gnostic of Islam," represented Arabic letters as not mere symbols of divine attributes, but God's actual body parts. Mughīra, in a case of what Steven Wasserstrom calls the "folk interconfessionalism of magicians," drew from a variety of resources that were in circulation around him, from Manicheans and Mandeans to Aramaic-speaking Jews and Christians as well as "various gnosticized pagans" in eighth-century Iraq.[22] As the charismatic leader of his own Mughirīyya movement, he reportedly went so far as to claim that God was a man of light who possessed a body made of Arabic letters and wore revealed scriptures as garments: the Qur'ān was God's loincloth, the Gospels his robes, the Torah his shirt, and the Psalms his pants.[23] For the Mughirīyya, God was not only anthropomorphic but scriptomorphic, embodying the sacredness of his language with his own limbs, while letters in turn became theomorphic and could now conjure images of the divine.

Interestingly (and ironically, given the term's later usage as a privileged Sunnī punching-down at Shī'ī communities), Mughīra is reported in some sources as being the first to disparage Shī'ī Muslims with the pejorative *rāfiḍa*, "rejecters," because they had rejected his own claim to Imāmic power.[24] The slur would then be appropriated by Sunnīs for use against Shī'īs over their denial of the first three caliphs.

Mughīra was ultimately executed and remembered in history as a sectarian heretic and imposter, but more established traditions preserved possibilities for graphemes, divine powers, and spiritually advanced seekers to interconnect. In a famous report, 'Alī ibn Abū Ṭālib is said to have declared that the heart of the Qur'ān was its first sūra, *al-Fātiḥa*, and the heart of *al-Fātiḥa* was its opening verse, *Bismillāhi-r-Raḥmāni-r-Raḥīm* ("In the Name of God, ar-Raḥmān, the Merciful"), and the heart of that verse was its first word, *Bismillāh*, and the heart of the *Bismillāh* was its first letter, ب, and the heart of the ب was its dot, and 'Alī himself was that dot—the heart of the heart of the heart of the heart of the heart of God's own eternal word. This statement cannot be historical ('Alī could not have described himself as the dot under a letter, since the Arabic script did not possess dots in his lifetime), but highlights the tradition's development of 'Alī as a transcendent being through his special connection to the Qur'ān. Investments in the Arabic alphabet can find support in the Qur'ān's own presentation of letters. Twenty-nine of the Qur'ān's 114 ṣūras begin with seemingly random assortments of *ḥurūf al-muqaṭṭa'a*, or "disconnected letters." The second ṣūra, for example, begins with the sequence ا, ل, م, which translators either render in transliteration as *alif, lām, mīm*, or as *A, L, M.* The letters appear in groupings up to five, and in some cases a ṣūra opens with a singular letter. At no point does the Qur'ān offer an explanation as to the purpose of these letters; ironically, the letters often show up near the Qur'ān's assertions of its clear and plain message.[25] Muslim thinkers throughout the centuries, as well as contemporary scholars, have postulated various theories on the meanings of the "mystery letters": allegorical readings held the letters as they appeared in particular sequences to be symbolic of divine attributes or the chain of transmission from God to Gabriel to Muḥammad; theologians who argued for the Qur'ān as having been created rather than eternal read the letters as pointing to the Qur'ān's appearance within bounded time; some interpreters considered the letters as a stylistic strategy to captivate the Qur'ān's original audience; scholars have even argued that the letters are not actually part of the Qur'ān itself, but rather a post-Muḥammad bibliography providing the initials of early Muslims who had memorized portions of the Qur'ān and contributed them to the canonical text.[26] According to Avicenna, the mystery letters act within the Qur'ān as a code indicating phases in which Allāh created the universe.[27] Devin Stewart argues that the mystery letters operate as "statements of mantic authority" that signal the Qur'ān's heavenly source.[28]

In their devotion to the Qur'ān as God's eternal speech—and interest in discovering its resources by which one might access unseen forces—readers of the Qur'ān that we would now call "esotericists," "occultists," or perhaps "magicians" carefully explored the sacred text for patterns and relationships. As Muslim thinkers of varying intellectual backgrounds developed sophisticated explorations of the letters, it would become more challenging to decide where letter-based "magic" ends and lettrist "mysticism" begins. Ja'fār al-Ṣādiq, sixth Imām in Shī'ī tradition, is represented in numerous narrations as an esotericist who possessed a vast knowledge of alphanumeric sciences that would be called occult or magical today. Ibn al-'Arabī, author of the "mystico-philosophical" *al-Futūhat al-Makkīyya*, presented letters in a hierarchical typology and elaborated on their special properties and connections to divine attributes; al-Būnī, author of the "popular and mystical" *Shams al-Ma'ārif*, discusses each Arabic letter as having its own secret characteristics, kingdoms, ruler, and servants.[29] Ibn al-'Arabī's opponents would denounce his overlaps with magicians and sorcerers, while al-Būnī is remembered today more as an authority on magic than as a Ṣūfī thinker. The treatment of Arabic words and letters as the building blocks of reality in texts marked "Ṣūfī" could indeed sound "magical"; meanwhile, the piety in a magical encyclopedia such as al-Būnī's *Shams*, grounded in the Ninety-nine Beautiful Names of God, does not typically earn it categorization as a theologically concerned or devotional text. Certainly Mughīra ibn Sa'īd, who imagined God as a man composed of Arabic letters, defies the binary: for Mughīra's skill as a juggler, we might place him on the side of magicians, while his claim to know Allāh's secret "Greatest Name" would position him as a mystic;[30] but does his claim to raise the dead constitute a magician's boast or a mystic's miracle? For some, the only difference would be whether he could really do it.

The Qur'ān's opening sūra, *al-Fātiḥa*, made for a natural point of focus for talisman makers, and its ingredients have been thoroughly examined by lettrist thinkers. The sūra consists of seven verses, resonating with the special significance accorded to the number seven across cultures and traditions in the Qur'ān's world. Of the twenty-eight letters in the Arabic alphabet, seven letters do not appear in the verses of *al-Fātiḥa*: these *sawāqitu-l-fātiḥa* consist of half of the fourteen "letters of darkness," letters associated with negative emotions and phenomena, such as hatred and war.[31] These letters were also held by talisman makers to each correspond to both a name of God and one of the seven "planets": ف = al-Fard and the Sun; ج = al-Jabbār and the Moon; ش = al-Shakūr and Mars; ز = al-Zakī and Saturn; ث = al-Thābit and Mercury; ظ = al-Ẓahīr and Jupiter; خ = al-Khabīr and Venus.[32]

Such divisions of Arabic letters into various classes and relationships would inform their uses in talismans: letters could be connected to each other based on their similar shapes, the number of letters required to write out their names, the number (or lack) of dots, or their appearances in God's names. (God's attribute of al-Qayyūm was said to be especially powerful because it contained the letters ق and م, both of which were believed to appear in God's secret Greatest Name.)[33]

For their special properties, Allāh's names are broken down into the letters that compose them and then integrated in amulets with the letters of a patient's name. Amulets have been known by a variety of names in the countless languages of Muslim-majority contexts; one Arabic term for amulet, *ḥijāb*, literally signifies "veiling" and expresses a metaphysical parallel to the ḥijāb of fabric. While the ḥijāb of fabric covers its wearer against unwelcome gazes, the ḥijāb of letters "covers" its wearer in a different way, providing a protective shield against malevolent energies and the *evil* eye.

The powers that could be accessed through letters could also be engaged with numbers. Letters and numbers directly related to each other in the system of *abjad*, in which letters were assigned numerical values. For the most part, these values corresponded to the letters' order (ب, for example, was the second letter of the Arabic alphabet, and thus valued at two), with some letters valued at multiples of ten or one hundred, and matched similar systems in older Semitic alphabets (though these consisted of fewer letters). The numerical equivalents for words and phrases could be used in their place: replacing a name with its numerical value could keep the name secret.[34] Both letters and numbers could be arranged in grids—termed "alphabetical squares" in the case of the former, "magic squares" in the latter—that were believed to hold special powers. In alphabetical squares, letters were arranged so that none of the rows or columns repeated. In magic squares, numbers were arranged so that every row and column produced the same sum. In some squares, letters could stand in for numbers, or vice versa; al-Būnī provides magic squares based on the numerical values of letters in specific jinns' names.[35] Though squares' opponents might regard them as siḥr, the squares are often expressions of conventional piety: besides jinns, angels, and planets, al-Būnī's collection includes squares based on Qur'ānic phrases and each of Allāh's ninety-nine names.[36]

For their relation to letters, numbers can function as prayers: hence the popular usage of 786, which in abjad values equals the letters that spell *Bismillāhir Raḥmānir Raḥīm*. In truck art or other mediums vulnerable to the dirt and defilement of the outside world, 786 could sacralize a space through the representation of Allāh's name while protecting the name itself from exposure. Though the written name is technically absent, its numerical equivalent can still transmit baraka.[37] Investments in the special qualities of letters and the correspondence of letters to numbers would contribute to both magical and mystical traditions, often blurring the distinction between them. Ja'far al-Ṣādiq, sixth Shī'ī Imām, would thus be associated in some circles with the teaching of arithmomancy. The great Muslim alchemist Jābir ibn Ḥayyān, who taught that material things could be comprehended by the letters and numerical values that composed their names, self-identified as a disciple of Ja'far al-Ṣādiq. Beyond their correspondences to letters, numbers could attain power from other associations. The number five, for example, became linked to defense against the evil eye for its resonance with the five fingers of the hand, which finds frequent representation as a protective charm: hanging from doors or necklaces, the open hand repels the evil eye, pushing negative energies back to their source. Though the hand-shaped amulet (*khamsa*, literally "five") in the Middle East predates Islam, popular Muslim usage reimagines the hand as that of 'Alī's son 'Abbās ibn 'Alī (who lost his hands and life leading Ḥusayn's army at the battle of Karbala) or more prominently Muḥammad's daughter Fāṭima. The number five has taken on such power that in some contexts, simply saying "khamsa" can express an effective curse.[38]

The notion of letters having secrets and transmitting their qualities into the names and words in which they appear would become salient for practices of divination, but also produce methods of interpreting scripture, treating divinely revealed text as a cipher to be unlocked, and attaining advanced spiritual knowledge. If the ق is no longer just a grapheme that Allāh combines with others to make his arguments and declarations, but also a unit of divine power through which Allāh created and maintains the universe, engaging the Qur'ān cannot be simply a scholarly enterprise. To open the book is to place oneself in direct encounter with devastating or illuminating energies that offer possibilities beyond mere comprehension. Lettrism, therefore, is where the categories of "magician" and "mystic" can sometimes reveal their absolute separation to be artificial. Both operate on ideas about the letters being eternal and uncreated cosmic entities that preexisted the world and which transmit divine knowledge and power through revealed scripture. One could argue that the paths diverge when the magician pursues knowledge of the letters for material benefit, while the mystic seeks to unlock the letters to achieve an advanced spiritual station and intensified closeness to God; but in both cases, mastery of the letters can contribute toward tangible effects in this world. The magician can use letters to protect their wearers against demons and disease, or even to help them win love; the mystic can be honored by God through the gift of *karamāt*, marvelous and miraculous acts that defy nature, and which are distinguished from the tricks or demonically assisted feats of sorcerers. But the average person, neither a mystic nor a magician, seeks out the blessed saint as well as the maker of amulets and talismans for identical purposes. Contact with holy people can heal the sick, even if the contact comes through visiting the saint's tomb. The amulet maker also provides a religious service, founded upon faith in the Qur'ān as a mode of accessing divine help. In both cases, knowledge of the letters and their secrets can qualify the practitioner as a specialist who provides valued services to flesh-and-blood bodies in their earthly lives.

Between the Letters

Even for Muslims who were not interested in mystical explorations of letters or indulgence in lettrist esotericisms, the written and vocalized reproductions of Allāh's eternal speech brought Muslims in closer relation to unseen powers. Muslims sometimes attempted to engage these powers through methods that were familiar in their contexts, hence the application of "pre-Islamic magic" to the Qur'ān. In Mesopotamia, for example, Muslim inscriptions of Qur'ānic verses onto drinking vessels mirrored the text-bearing "magic bowls" that had been popular in the region for centuries prior to Islam.[39] Lettrism is perhaps less a side effect of belief in divine scripture and more a technology, like the paper technology on which it is written, that can be appropriated anywhere and manipulated for its users' specific needs. Therefore, while it seems intuitive to make reductionist claims about Muslim lettrisms as entirely driven by values *within* Islam—such as faith in the Qur'ān as eternal divine speech—the truth is that confidence in the power of words to produce observable change upon lived reality was not a unique result of Muslim beliefs. The first Muslims in any premodern setting, whether the original community of the Arabian Peninsula or the early waves of converts in settings such as Iran, India, or the Sudan, believed in this relationship of language to the world before they became Muslims. As much as the Qur'ān could have informed and inspired pursuits of metaphysical powers in words and letters, the Qur'ān as a concept could also be considered a result of the worldviews in which these beliefs were possible. The Qur'ān could not have been accepted as supernaturally authored unless words already had the power to be more than words, to enter into the world through metaphysical forces and intervene in the lives of humans.

Rather than look at shared practices as acts of "borrowing" or "copying" that expose these Muslims as inauthentic or their religiosity as lacking integrity, perhaps we should ask what such practices express in terms of shared general assumptions about the nature of language. Belief in the power of words to affect material reality crosses religious borders. Reproductions of divine language make an obvious choice for selection as tools, cures, shields, or perhaps even weapons. While readers of the Qur'ān perceived it through the lens of a world in which words were understood to carry real power and do *magical* things, Muslims were not only passive receivers of magical lettrism, but actively contributed to lettrist traditions. The exchanges and collaborations between Muslim and Jewish lettrisms in late antique and early medieval Iraq, along with the lasting magical and mystical legacies emerging from these encounters, contribute toward an unraveling of the common "Clash of Civilization" narratives that pit an alien "Islamic World" against a "Judeo-Christian West." These representations imagine Islam and the West as two eternally isolated and antithetical civilizations that can either achieve peace or destroy each other in war, but never truly comingle. There are multiple ways of challenging the Clash of Civilizations myth; one strategy points to overlaps and intersections throughout history that demonstrate these supposedly separate civilizations to have been consistently embedded in one another. This can be done by examining the intellectual exchanges between Muslims, Christians, and Jews in traditions of philosophy, theology, and science, contributing to a counternarrative in which such lofty pursuits represent collaborations and a shared heritage between diverse traditions. It could perhaps also be achieved with a look at the less prestigious tradition of letter magic, which also crosses all imagined borders between various cultural, religious, and geographic categories—so much so that we have evidence of medieval Jewish amulets that bear witness to Muḥammad's prophethood and use the Qur'ānic formula *bismillāh*, "In the name of God."[40]

As the source of its own magical lettrism, the Qur'ān becomes something of a paradox: it acts as a resolutely anti-magical text, making every effort to distance itself from siḥr, but nonetheless remains a source of magical energies between its covers, performing magic of its own while fighting magic on magic's terms. The Qur'ān proves itself to be greater than magic by outperforming magic on its own claims. In lived tradition, this flow of energies in and through the Qur'ān could be as significant as its rhetoric. To conceptualize the Qur'ān as only a collection of discourse and persuasive argumentation, a resource for jurists and theologians, is almost to secularize the Qur'ān and reduce Allāh's eternal speech to a book like any book.

Someone working from a certain set of ideas about "authentic" Islam and where we could find it might raise the objection that esoteric or magical lettrists are projecting their own ideas and materials onto the Qur'ān, mixing the Qur'ān with outside sources, which enables them to distort or even deny what's actually being said *inside* the Qur'ān. This is certainly fair. On the other hand, to disqualify some readers for viewing the text within their own culturally specific sciences and unquestioned assumptions seems to risk undue confidence that *we* have transcended all of the prevailing prejudices and epistemological assumptions that govern our own contexts, and that we read the text with no interference from cultures beyond its pages—that we see the Qur'ān objectively and purely for *what it is* and *what it says*. Some readers of the Qur'ān will pursue its "true" message within the frameworks of a particular Sunnī or Shī'ī neotraditionalism or postmodernist literary theories of the secular academy; others will take for granted that a natural correspondence exists between the first letter in the Arabic word for "killing" and the actual forces that end a life. If we don't intuitively expect such a correspondence, it doesn't mean that we simply read the book as it really is, but only that we throw a different accumulation of baggage upon its words.

It is easy to assert, as scholars have already done, that Islam as presented by the marvel-worker and mystic Mughīra was "barely Islamic" and that various aspects of his teachings betray origins in non-Islamic materials. Mughīra could have learned his letter elementalism, theology of embodied anthropomorphism, and cosmological system from other resources available in eighth-century Iraq; his eclectic use of sources seems to have been used against him, as Shī'ī Imām Ja'far al-Ṣādiq accused Mughīra of studying siḥr under the tutelage of a Jewish woman.[41] But regardless of his influences and the resources available to him, Mughīra had also disseminated his own interpretive commentary on the Qur'ān, in which he brought his worldviews to bear upon Muslims' divine revelation. In his commentary, according to a ninth-century Mu'tāzilī intellectual, Mughīra conceptualized the Qur'ān as "entirely composed of symbols and cryptic hints" for which humanity depended on his knowledge to unlock the text.[42] The God-Man who was composed of Arabic letters had revealed with the Qur'ān a self-disclosure in the very forms of his body. Whether someone wants to call Mughīra a Muslim mystic or heretical sorcerer, he expressed a commitment to the Qur'ān that we cannot judge to have been insincere or illegitimate simply because it looks weird or unsophisticated to us. Mughīra's limitation as an interpreter seems to be that he approached the Qur'ān with eyes that a particular set of sources had made for him, and that he found meaning in the Qur'ān through the culturally specific experience of it that his world had made possible. Can any of us claim better for ourselves?

4

The Stars Are Muslims

> No, I swear by the locations of the stars.
>
> —QUR'ĀN 56:75

The Qur'ān frequently begins sūras with oaths in which the authorial voice swears by various phenomena, such as the sun, the moon, the mountains, galloping horses, or time itself. The fifty-third sūra begins with the oath, "By the star as it falls." The sūra then goes on to assure the community that its companion, Muḥammad, does not speak from his own desire, but rather divine instruction. The fifty-third sūra is characterized in part by its polemics against goddess worship, listing specific goddesses by name. It was also during the revelation of this sūra that the "Satanic Verses" incident was alleged to have taken place, in which Muḥammad reportedly misidentified verses from the Devil as coming from God, and briefly compromised the monotheism of his mission with a positive recognition of the goddesses.

The imagery of the falling star is compelling if one reflects on the possible prevalence of star worship in pre-Islamic Arabia. The fifty-third sūra, popularly known as *al-Najm*, "*The Star*," mentions one star in particular: al-Shi'ra, which corresponded to Sirius, the Dog Star (53:49). The verse, appearing within a sequence of verses in which Allāh asserts his absolute control over creation, life, death, laughter, tears, and the fates of nations, could be translated as, "and he is the Lord of Sirius." The Qur'ān does not contextualize Allāh's claim over Sirius or provide us with adequate material to realize its full consequences for the sūra's original audience; outside sources do not give much concrete information on the star's significance in pre-Islamic Arabia, but there is an implication that it was one of the celestial bodies associated with goddess worship. Without getting overly speculative, we can gather that the Qur'ān compels anyone who holds feelings of awe for Sirius to redirect their focus instead to the one who rules that star. Whatever Sirius might have meant to people in seventh-century Mecca, it had a lord of its own.

The ḥadīth corpus contains more explicit denunciations of astral religion. Muḥammad is reported as stating that whenever Allāh bestows favor upon a group of people, there are disbelievers who attribute these blessings not to Allāh, but to the stars. Some ḥadīth reports specifically mention people claiming that the stars give rain, and make it clear that believing in God means disbelieving in the stars. To grant the stars a causative role in earthly affairs, according to these ḥadīths, means that one has failed to recognize God's absolute sovereignty. The ḥadīth reports are further supplemented by other claims on Meccan religion before the rise of Islam. Ninth-century traditionist Ibn Qutayba cited pre-Islamic poetry in which the risings and settings of stars were perceived as having a bearing on rain periods, and twelfth-century scholar al-Zamakhsharī's commentary on the fifty-third sūra asserts that the goddess Manat was connected to astral worship and beseeched for rain in the pre-Islamic period. Daniel Martin Varisco explains that while some pre-Islamic Arabs indeed prayed to stars for rain, "others simply used the observation of stars to mark the probable times of rains."[1]

Does the ḥadīth corpus draw a binary of its own between astral religion and astral magic? Ḥadīth traditions warn against assigning power to the stars, but it can be questioned whether the ḥadīth corpus makes an absolute conflation between astrolatry (the worship of stars as gods) and astrology (the study of celestial phenomena to find meaning in their relations to each other and earthly affairs). In ḥadīth sources, Muḥammad appears to have prohibited his followers from engaging the stars as a source of information, and associated such pursuits with demonically oriented practices: A well-reported tradition found in the most trusted ḥadīth volumes quotes Muḥammad as having said, "Whoever acquires knowledge from the stars, acquires knowledge of siḥr, and gets more as long as he continues to do so." But another ḥadīth, appearing in Bukhārī's supremely prestigious *Ṣaḥīḥ*, portrays Muḥammad's own arrival as foretold by a Christian emperor's practice of astrology. The Roman king Heraclius, depicted in this narrative as a skilled astrologer, learned from his observations of the stars that an anticipated "king of the circumcised" was about to appear on the world stage. A member of the court advised that Heraclius should issue orders for every Jew in the empire to be killed, since they were the only ones to practice circumcision. Upon learning that Arabs also engaged in circumcision, Heraclius realized that the time for their sovereignty was imminent. Within the same immense canon, we find Muḥammad condemning astrology within the broader category of siḥr—an offense that other statements attributed to Muḥammad designate as punishable by death—and astrology providing a proof of Muḥammad's special place in human destiny. What does it mean if astral siḥr was a prohibited sin but still granted its practitioners knowledge of a blessed prophet? Finally, did it make a difference if the stars were perceived as mere signifiers of God's plan unfolding, rather than as causes with their own power and agency? Elsewhere in the ḥadīth corpus, Muḥammad simultaneously rejects the treatment of celestial phenomena as texts to be read for meaning and confesses to their significance. He denies that the sun and moon could eclipse in relation to someone's birth or death, but also treats an eclipse as a sign of Allāh that warrants its own special prayers and supplications until the eclipse has ended. There are also narrations in which Muḥammad displays divinely revealed knowledge of celestial secrets: according to one tradition, when a Jewish challenger promises to become Muslim if only Muḥammad can name the eleven stars from Joseph's dream, Muḥammad remains silent until learning the names from Gabriel: al-Ṭāriq, al-Dhiyāl, Dhū'l-Katfayn, Qābis, Withāb, 'Amūdān, al-Falīq, Al-Ḍurūḥ, Dhū-l-Faragh, al-Ḍiyā', and al-Nūr.[2] In this report, Muḥammad appears as the acceptable mirror to unacceptable astrologers. He does the same work—authorizing himself by privileged knowledge of celestial bodies—but receives his information from a proper source, the angel of revelation, rather than a jinn or demon. Muslim traditions also establish Muḥammad's special nature through his association with celestial signs, most prominently the miraculous "splitting of the Moon."

As Robert G. Morrison has observed in examinations of early

Qur'ān commentaries, the notion that God used celestial bodies as instruments in his control over creation was not at all radical.[3] In later interpretive traditions, we encounter the same simultaneous appearances of astrology's prohibition with recognition of its possible legitimacy. The great fourteenth-century sociologist Ibn Khaldūn offered a number of arguments on behalf of astrology's divinely ordered prohibition, ranging from the theological (only God has any power to cause events) to sociological (astrologers are harmful to the public welfare) to theoretical (even if astrology were a valid science, life is too short for anyone to acquire sufficient mastery of this immeasurably vast field to actually make use of it).[4] But even while refuting astrology, Ibn Khaldūn admitted that stars could conceivably influence earthly events; this itself was not a radical statement in the science of his world. He even stated that perfect astral conjunctions were a necessary prerequisite for the appearance of prophets, and that imperfect conjunctions would result in only crude diviners.[5]

Inconsistency or ambiguity in response to astrology is not uniquely a Muslim phenomenon. In Jewish traditions, prohibitions of astrology coexist alongside the realities of lived practice, as well as prevailing premodern sciences that informed nuanced philosophical reflections. The relationship of celestial bodies to earthly events is taken for granted everywhere, from "folk religion," as in Mesopotamian magic bowls; to sectarian communities, as in evidence of the Qumran community's dabbling in astral sciences; to worldviews taken for granted by elite intellects such as Philo as facts of nature.[6] A Jewish "Book of Mysteries" from the early centuries CE promises to divulge secret instructions for investigating the seven-tiered heaven and understanding the movements of bodies such as the sun, moon, and constellations. It even offers the modes of accessing these bodies' angelic or divine attendants: knowledge of their names, preferences for oblations, and the times at which they hear prayer and answer those who call to them.[7] In the *Testament of Solomon*, the angel Michael delivers a seal ring to Solomon, which gives Solomon the power to subjugate demons and compel them to reveal their zodiacal positions; there are even legends in which Abraham teaches astrology. Accounts in Talmudic literature exempt Israel from absolute astral determinism but also leave openings for astrology to remain valid as a science.[8]

Christian traditions likewise abound with ambiguities concerning knowledge of the stars. A source of profound Christian tension over astrology's legitimacy could even be found in the New Testament, as the Gospel of Matthew mentions Zoroastrian priests (magi) who were alerted to Christ's birth through their science of reading the stars. The most vehement Christian opponents of astrology still had to contend with a star heralding the arrival of their Messiah, and so a variety of seminal Christian thinkers offered denials of astrology that included some negotiations with its power. Tertullian, for example, attributed astrology to fallen angels who taught the science to humans, granting astrology a supernatural origin that was nonetheless the wrong one.[9] Some argued that the nativity star's appearance demonstrated that Christ's arrival meant the conclusion of astrology, since his birth caused such immense effects in the heavens that stars were shaken from their regular movements and astrologers could no longer rely on stars' courses for their predictions. The argument also appeared that while stars still ruled over the lives of non-Christians, those who accepted baptism in Christ were liberated from the fetters of astral fatalism.[10] Polytheists, meanwhile, made use of the nativity star in their anti-Christian arguments, since it demonstrated that not only Christians, but even Christ himself remained subject to polytheist traditions.[11] Regardless of Christian or polytheist thinkers presenting astrology as a non-Christian (or, more charitably, pre-Christian) field, Christian sources also reveal Christians in the early centuries of the Common Era practicing astrology, even striving to perform baptism only on astrally auspicious days.[12] On the other side, anti-astrology Christians did not only argue against astrology with expressly Christian or biblical tools, but often recycled criticisms of astrology that were first raised by polytheist philosophers.[13]

When we consider the full historical complexity within Jewish and Christian treatments of astrology, it becomes impossible to imagine early Muslim thought as torn between "Abrahamic" and "Hellenic" perspectives, or present some Muslims as effectively defending an insulated "Abrahamic tradition" against infiltrations from outside sources—even if this was the claim that they made for themselves. The history of Jewish and Christian astrology, if we want to imagine astrology as coming from "outside," shows that there was never really an outside. First, the texts and opinions that eventually attain power as canon and orthodoxy do not represent the entirety of a tradition or grant us the luxury of silencing all other voices. Second, a careful look at those canonical scriptures and authoritative opinions reveals much more diversity and dynamic conversations than many would expect to see. This means that even if we limit ourselves to classic rabbinical literatures and the writings of the church fathers, we are not going to uncover *the* singular and clear "Jewish position" or "Christian position" on astrology. The illusory monolith of Abrahamic tradition, let alone a singular Abrahamic view of astrology, was already hybrid and internally incoherent long before Muḥammad's movement or the multiplicity of voices that would claim it.

While these traditions are always characterized by exchange, we can speak of an especially monumental encounter that would transform Muslim intellectualism forever. From shortly after the 'Abbāsid revolution in the mid–seventh century through the end of the tenth century, an ambitious state-supported translation project rendered mountains of Persian, Indian, and Greek literatures accessible in Arabic. The translated works covered seemingly every conceivable topic, from natural science and medicine to mathematics to history to philosophy and theology.[14] As Baghdad became a global center of premodern learning, Muslim thinkers actively engaged a variety of scientific and philosophical heritages. The resultant speculations, debates, and sectarian antagonisms that emerged from this intellectual activity impacted Muslim thinkers, whether they wholeheartedly embraced and advocated new literatures and systems or sought effective borders between their understanding of uncorrupted Islam and the threat of outside theories and methods. Those pious traditionalists who opposed astrology as contrary to Islam were no less informed by "outside" sources than astrology's advocates. Fourteenth-century theologian Ibn Qayyim al-Jawziyya, for example, is recognized as one of the most influential intellectuals of the Ḥanbalī school, which is alternately praised or detested for its claims to staunchly defend "true" Islam against all forms of corruption and deviation. The Ḥanbalī school today enjoys official prestige in the modern Saudi state, and provides a premodern foundation for modern Sunnī revivalisms such as the Salafī and "Wahhābī" movements. In his refutation of astrology, Ibn Qayyim does use sacred history as proof, citing incidents in which astrologers predicted 'Alī's doom, but 'Alī triumphed due to his placing trust in God alone. However, Ibn Qayyim also takes on the astrologers with a rationalist attack grounded in Aristotelian cosmology, demonstrating the elusive nature of epistemological purity.[15]

Among the bodies of literature that entered into Arabic during the 'Abbāsid translation project were works of astrology, alchemy, and other "occult sciences."[16] Muslims responded to these works in a variety of ways. Certainly, just as in the case of Aristotelian and Neoplatonist concepts, some Muslim scholars rejected them on theological grounds. Others found the truths of these newly translated works confirmed by the heritage of the Qur'ān and Muḥammad, or vice versa. Whether Muslims opposed or embraced "foreign" bodies of knowledge, it would be naïve to imagine some Muslims as preserving the self-contained integrity of Islam by pushing away non-Islamic materials and their supposed opposites as producing a Hellenic-Islamic syncretism. The results were far more complex.

This seems like a good place to mention the problem of "influence." Sometimes, discussion of the 'Abbāsid translation project and resultant Muslim study of Greek philosophical, scientific, and occult literatures describes Muslim thinkers as passively influenced by these works. When considering the relationship between a dead author and living reader, however, perhaps we see "influence" moving the wrong direction. The reader is the one who picks up a book and makes it do things. Another way of imagining the encounter would prioritize the reader's active and creative engagement of the text, which does not merely receive meaning from the page but in fact *produces* it.

Claiming and Contesting Astrology

The mighty defender of what he constructed as Sunnī orthodoxy against rationalist philosophers, Abū Hāmid al-Ghazālī (d. 1111), regarded astrology as a knowledge that some prophets had been granted by God, but that could not be claimed by contemporary practitioners; his foremost objection was that belief in the stars as causes denied God's prestige as the only cause.[17] For many theologically driven opponents of astrology, to grant the stars a role in determining earthly events compromised God's absolute sovereignty. In the theological controversies of the earliest Muslim centuries, belief in human free will became a doctrinal point over which some Muslims—whose views ultimately triumphed in becoming privileged Sunnī "orthodoxy"—were willing to denounce others as having transgressed the limits of Islam. For advocates of this occasionalist perspective, God is the only doer in the universe. Statements attributed to Muḥammad in the ḥadīth corpus present him as condemning not only the notion of stars or other celestial bodies acting as determinants of earthly events, but also belief in evil omens, the "death bird" (*hāma*), and even contagious disease, along with human efforts to ascertain the future from studying the flights of birds or analyzing pebbles.[18]

From the many thousands of reports of Muḥammad's sayings and actions in the ḥadīth corpus, it appears to be self-evident that Muḥammad prohibited astrology and regarded belief in the stars' agency or power as disbelief in Allāh. Ḥadīth narrations are not necessarily inauthentic, and rigorous contemporary scholarship argues that wholesale rejection of the canonical corpus as a project of mass forgery is no more defensible than an uncritical acceptance of the canon as being entirely what it claims to be.[19] While recognizing that these statements attributed to Muḥammad *could* very well have come from his own mouth (but without absolute confidence that traditional evaluation of a narration's reporters could answer that question for us), we can also recognize that the ḥadīth corpus *as we access it* emerged in the same milieu as the translation movement and the variety of theological controversies that accompanied it. The ḥadīth corpus contains narrations in which Muḥammad appears to pronounce judgments on sectarian groups, tribal and imperial dynamics, and divisions within Muslims that did not exist in his own lifetime. Perhaps, being a prophet, he anticipated all of these things and could speak on the future; or these narrations could come from ideologues projecting their own arguments onto the prophetic voice. A ḥadīth in Bukhārī's *Ṣaḥīḥ* regarding astrology, therefore, *could* provide us with details concerning how astrology was conceptualized in seventh-century Arabia; at the very least, it tells us about the theological anxieties and sectarian debates of ninth-century Iraq. One point of consideration for the latter would be the Qur'ān's silence on astrology. We do not have conclusive evidence of astrology having been practiced in pre-Islamic Arabia; the Qur'ān mentions human beings using stars as a means of navigation, but says nothing explicitly concerning the study of stars' movements for divination. One could speculate that astrology only became a point of contention as Muslim territory expanded beyond the Hejāz into the broader Mediterranean and Persian contexts.

Ḥadīth scholars might have asserted with confidence that they possessed clear statements from Muḥammad himself on the sinfulness of astrology, but not all Muslim intellectuals of the early centuries held equal stock in the ḥadīth scholars' authority. In the ninth century CE, ḥadīth partisans constituted a sectarian group—the *Ahl al-Ḥadīth*, or "Ḥadīth Folk"—that maintained popular grassroots support and a complex relationship to the state, and could be seen as a nucleus for what would eventually become a Sunnī communal consciousness. By no means, however, could they wield the unquestioned privilege and tradition-making authority that their Sunnī heirs claim today. They were not the only game in town, and other Muslim thinkers could challenge their ḥadīth-centered methodology through other sources and modes of knowledge. If the Ḥadīth Folk condemned the science of astral relations to earthly events, and even named their condemnation as the divinely guided personal judgment of Muḥammad, it was possible to get a second opinion.

Roughly two centuries before al-Ghazālī condemned astrology as *kufr*, Abū Yūsuf Ya'qūb ibn Isḥāq al-Kindī (d. 870) presented astrology as highlighting the submission of the entire universe to God. Al-Kindī, who worked at the center of an "al-Kindī circle" of scholars and translators, counted among his students Abū Ma'shar, whom A. Azfar Moin calls the "father of Islamic astrology."[20] Reports charged that Abū Ma'shar was originally a ḥadīth scholar until al-Kindī dazzled him with geometry and arithmetic, which became gateways into astrology—which Abū Ma'shar studied until it in turn led him to become an atheist, thus suggesting atheism to be the inevitable result of astrological or even mathematical pursuits.[21] Another narrative even reported that Abū Ma'shar had been tempted toward astrology and away from conventional piety during his pilgrimage to Mecca, showing just how threatening this illicit science could be to the welfare of believers' hearts and souls.[22]

Al-Kindī, however, found astrology to be not only consistent with his Muslim faith, but a source of confirmation for its claims. Considered the first philosopher to write in Arabic, Al-Kindī also produced a considerable amount of scientific and theological writings in which Aristotle, Plotinus, and the Qur'ān could all enter into conversation with one another and largely manage to agree. "Since al-Kindī was in the business of advertising the power and truth of Greek philosophy," writes Peter Adamson, "he was predisposed to see all of ancient thought as a single, coherent system."[23] This coherence resonated with his theology's emphasis on transcendent divine unity, conveyed in Arabic as *tawḥīd*—a unity that he observed in the stars. Al-Kindī, while upholding the Qur'ān as the revealed word of God, also subscribed to Greek cosmologies and accepted the influence of celestial spheres on the earth as a fact of natural science. For al-Kindī, there was no conflict between these knowledges. For the stars' movements to cause events on the earth did not deny Allāh as the ultimate cause, but rather affirmed Allāh's complete mastery over all things. Astrology was not astrolatry, the worship of stars as gods with their own powers, even if al-Kindī believed the stars to possess rational souls. Rather, the effects of celestial bodies upon the earth offered a proof of Allāh's divine unity; in studying the movements of the stars and their correspondences to patterns in earthly events, al-Kindī found a science by which one could bear witness to Allāh's control over all worlds and bodies, which related to each other harmoniously in accordance with divine plan. As *The Theology of Aristotle*, held to have been authored by someone in the al-Kindī coterie, asserts, the stars "govern the earthly world in another way, not through a device or through thought or reflection, but rather through the power which the first originator and governor, may he be exalted, puts in them."[24]

Al-Kindī even supported his construction of pious astrology

with quotations from the Qur'ān, which describes the heavens as prostrating before God. The heavens and everything that they contain move by God's command in ways that will properly affect our world to achieve whatever God desires for it. Al-Kindī approached the stars not merely as a scientist or occultist in modern terms, but as a philosopher and theologian as well, seeking to answer the consequences of a universe in which celestial movements impacted earthly good and evil. Al-Kindī upheld divine sovereignty over all things. In his system, God remained in charge, even if al-Kindī used astrological methods to determine when God was most likely to answer prayers.[25]

If Allāh is indeed the Lord of Sirius, studying the star's movements and its relationships to the rest of creation provides another means of observing God's power. Of course, the suggestion that the heavens and earth were interrelated and equally under the control of their Creator was not itself theologically threatening. The Qur'ān exegesis of al-Ṭabarī even presents the heavens and earth as directly connected and held together by countless ropes "finer than hair and stronger than iron" that are invisible but present everywhere, allowing for some degree of causal relations and a mode by which human and superhuman personalities alike might ascend or descend.[26] Celestial bodies are only parts within the machinery by which divine plan runs, and they perform their functions in full obedience. The stars are Muslims.

Imperial/Islamic Astrologies

The 'Abbāsid translation movement is typically remembered today for its contributions to intellectual histories that are still taken seriously—namely, fields like philosophy, theology, biology, medicine, mathematics, and natural sciences, including astronomy. However, projecting contemporary assumptions about legitimate fields of study onto the 'Abbāsid period would leave some things out; the caliphal translation project could also be considered in modern terms as having an occult or esoteric dimension. As Hayrettin Yücesoy explains, medieval sources present the wisdom of the ancients as "associated with manuscripts, concealed libraries, scripts, and magical tablets either lying buried in ruins or kept in palaces, temples, and monasteries until they were discovered by and revealed to the deserving seeker."[27] Sources present the caliph al-Ma'mūn as this special seeker, having been guided toward the textual heritage of the past by Aristotle's appearance to him in a dream. Scholars warn against treating the dream as a cause of the translation movement; the dream was more likely a product of it.[28] But Yücesoy offers a convincing speculation of al-Ma'mūn's project as driven by a growing matrix of fables and legends about hidden or protected sacred knowledge that would today cross back and forth between our categories of magic, religion, and science. Especially provocative is the consideration of al-Ma'mūn's excavations of the pyramid of Cheops, which astrologer Abū Ma'shar believed to have been an antediluvian archive and which other legends associated with Qur'ānic prophets such as Adam or Idrīs.[29] While some Muslim temporal and spiritual authorities reviled pharaonic Egypt as a legacy of pre-Islamic *jahiliyya* (ignorance), idolatry, and oppression (Pharaoh stands as the Qur'ān's paradigmatic tyrant) and called for the destruction of its material heritage—such as Saladin's son al-Azīz, who attempted to destroy the pyramids, and a fourteenth-century Ṣūfī named Muḥammad Sa'im ad-Dahr, who destroyed the Sphinx's nose because Muslim peasants had been offering prayers and sacrifices to it—numerous premodern Muslims recognized Egypt's pre-Islamic past as one of advanced knowledge and wisdom. Some even included astrology as part of this heritage. Abū 'Ubayd al-Bakrī wrote in the eleventh century that the ancient Egyptians attributed their own advancement to what they had learned from celestial bodies. He cites "the wisest Greeks" as testifying that the "wise men of Egypt" credited astrology for their civilization, for "it was the stars that taught them the secrets of the nature of things." For their highly developed technologies of soothsaying, talismans, and reading the stars, the wise men of Egypt "begat children who spoke at birth" and also produced "pictures that moved."[30]

Astrologers enjoyed some access to political privilege in the 'Abbāsid caliphate, as caliphs sought their consultations when strategizing politically or undertaking major projects such as the construction of Baghdad. Al-Manṣūr (d. 775) laid the foundations of Baghdad on Friday, July 30, 762 (or the fourth day of Jumāda al-Awāl, 145), due to the calculations of his court astrologers.[31] One of the consultants in this project was famed Persian Jewish astrologer Mashā'allāh. In addition to determining an auspicious date for the founding of Baghdad, Mashā'allāh served the court with his analysis of historical events, including the reigns of caliphs and even the Prophet's own mission.[32] Among the resources in Mashā'allāh's astrological toolbox was the Jupiter-Saturn conjunction theory from pre-Islamic Sassanian Persia, which presented time as cyclical and held Jupiter and Saturn to be the drivers of human history.[33] Astrological analysis also successfully predicted the ascension of al-Ma'mūn to the caliphate, proving God's favor for al-Ma'mūn and securing a place for court astrologers in his regime.[34] Astrology even factored into imperial medicine, as Bukhtīshū' ibn Jibrīl (d. 870), physician to three 'Abbāsid caliphs in Baghdad, gave orders for medicine to be taken only when the Moon aligned with Venus, and also based his prescriptions of enemas on the Moon's position.[35]

It reads as a bit ironic that while Ismā'īlī tradition is derided by many Sunnī Muslims as overly esotericist to the point of leaving Islam altogether, astrologers in the Ismā'īlī Fāṭimid caliphate did not reach the heights of access to power that they enjoyed in the Sunnī (or proto-Sunnī) 'Abbāsid caliphate. While Ismā'īlī scholars made use of astrology to calculate the arrival of the expected messianic hero, and caliphates did have court astrologers, the Fāṭimids also issued decrees banning astrology. The caliph al-'Azīz had a court astrologer, but ultimately rejected him for the pro-Sunnī elements in his astrological reading of history.[36] Reports concerning the founding of Cairo even memorialize a Fāṭimid disavowal of astrology within the city's name. Court astrologers reportedly gave warning of an inauspicious conjunction of Mars and Virgo, which the leadership ignored and proceeded to conquer/found the city with complete success. The city was then named al-Qāhira, which celebrated the Fāṭimid victory with God's attribute of al-Qāhir, "the Victorious"—and also spited the naysaying astrologers (or deflected the omen's threat), since al-Qāhir happened to be the name for Mars. Fāṭimid caliph al-Manṣūr, who reigned from 946 to 953, admitted to having studied astrology, but asserted that it was only because astrology leads to the "confession of the oneness of God and the effects of his wisdom on the deeds of his creation."[37] The caliph rejected astrology as a means of divination because its predictions often contradicted visions of the future that had been revealed to his heart, and his heart always turned out to be right.[38]

Later Muslim empires continued to employ astrologers as consultants and even shapers of state ideology: as Moin notes in his discussion of Safavid, Timurid, and Mughal notions of mystical or sacred kingship, "astrology was as 'political' a science as history" in terms of its power to legitimize a state.[39] Astrological findings, just like any statistics in the modern world, could be interpreted, manipulated, and even fabricated to serve either side of a political struggle. The conjunction of Saturn and Jupiter, the "superior planets," and the cyclical readings of time inspired by its appearances became an especially useful resource for making power claims and positioning kings as divinely mandated. Claiming an astrally authorized mandate to rule did not distance the king from Islam, but could be read in Muslim terms, since God was still lord of the stars and celestial bodies. Boasting of a connection to the Saturn-Jupiter conjunction could even relate a king to Muḥammad: the Prophet himself, according to an astrologer, was born under the Saturn-Jupiter conjunction.[40] The schedule of Mughal emperor Humayun's court, organized in accordance with the relationships between planets and days of the week, names Saturday and Thursday as the days for the king to meet with advisers regarding knowledge and religious devotion; this is because Saturday relates to Saturn, "protector of shaykhs and ancient lineages," and Thursday relates to Jupiter, "the planet of the Prophet's family and religious scholars."[41] There is no sign of tension here between "Islam" and "astrology" as separate traditions being forced into conversation; this could be called "Islamic astrology," though some would be mortified at the idea. Likewise, Humayun's division of his court into twelve ranks drew its justification not only from the proliferation of the number twelve in the Qur'ān and Muslim traditions (such as the twelve Imāms of Ithna Ash'arī Shī'ism), but also the twelve signs of the Zodiac.[42]

In modern Muslim discourses, theorizations of an "Islamic state" do not consider astrology as one of the necessary elements in the blueprint for a perfectly Islam-centered government. Throughout Muslim histories, however, empires claiming to represent Islam were ruled by mystical, charismatic, *messianic* sacred kings whose special places in human destiny and divine plan were signaled by the stars and planets. To make such a case for their claims to divinely endorsed power, numerous kings referred to the truth-making authority of astrology, which Moin calls a "global science" in premodernity. Identification as "Lords of Conjunction" did not signal these sacred kings' betrayal of Islam, but rather authorized them as faithful heirs to the Prophet, a Lord of Conjunction himself; and finding one's reign written in the stars only confirmed that victory had been decided by God.

Ascended Masters: Celestial Bodies and Prophetic Journeys

Throughout Muslim traditions, the story of Muḥammad's journey through the seven heavens, meeting different prophets at each tier before finally having an encounter with God, has provoked a seemingly endless archive of devotional literatures, commentaries, mystical speculations, and artistic representations. The ascension's presentation of seven heavens often undergoes a transformation in the hands of modern readers, even without a second thought: the seven heavens are reconceptualized as a "religious" fact, safely separate from trespassing upon the "secular" facts of science. The seven-tiered heaven is understood as referring to the reality of another dimension, *beyond* physical creation, rather than something comprehensible in this universe with our modern technologies of observation. While premodern literatures do exist in which the ascension is treated in allegorical terms or taken to represent an inward journey (an account attributed to Muḥammad's wife 'Ā'isha insists that the journey took place in a dream, and that Muḥammad's body never left Mecca on the night in question), the division between "secular"/"scientific" and "religious" ideas of the heavens was not always legible. For the insistence that Muḥammad's ascension was indeed fully embodied—which ultimately became the dominant narrative over claims of dreams or visions—the story tracks a man's physical journey through the actual, material universe as many people perceived the universe to have been organized.

The seven heavens visited by Muḥammad corresponded to ways in which traditional cosmologies understood the structure of the universe. The ascension was depicted in conformity to the science of its time, which imagined the earth at the center of concentric celestial spheres that each corresponded to a known "planet": the Moon, Mercury, Venus, the Sun, Mars, Jupiter, and Saturn. Commentators seeking to investigate the deeper meanings of Muḥammad's experiences and interactions at each sphere of the heavens did not treat the ascension as a purely "Islamic" artifact to be isolated from other fields of knowledge, but read the ascension through those fields.

If Muḥammad met the prophet Jesus at the second heaven, for example, interpreters of the ascension would consider how Jesus might relate to the properties of the planet Mercury, the celestial body associated with that heaven. If Muḥammad encountered

Abraham at the seventh heaven before transcending the spheres to have an audience with God beyond the entire structure, and Saturn was the planet associated with the seventh heaven, this suggested a correspondence of some kind between Abraham and Saturn. Just as Muslim intellectuals today might use findings of modern science to retrieve a wealth of new meanings from verses of the Qur'ān, or even to prove the Qur'ān's status as divine revelation to skeptics, premodern Muslims read the Qur'ān and Muḥammad's life through the sciences of their own age, some of which would be considered more occult or metaphysical than legitimate "science" today.

For his ascension through the successive layers of heavens, Muḥammad took part in a literary genre that was widespread throughout the Mediterranean and Persian milieus of late antiquity. These journeys of holy men upward into the skies often deny our modern separations of religion and science, since these narratives often served to explain human awareness of astronomy: a privileged adept ascends into the heavens, a construction where divine and material knowledges intersect, and the adept receives knowledge of how the universe operates—which makes a claim on knowledge of both the seen and unseen realms.[43] For this reason, Ithamar Gruenwald writes that in prophetic ascension narratives, "there was no substantial difference between religion, philosophy, and science."[44]

Muḥammad's ascension through the successive layers of heavens has been read in conversation with preexisting ideas of this world as a golden apple's rotten core: Muḥammad fulfilled the philosophers' quest of transcending the rotten core and escaping into the gold. The goal of the philosopher was to ascend back through the spheres to reunite with the origin of existence, essentially pursuing through rigorous intellectual training the kind of personal perfection that came naturally and intuitively to prophets. It was also the Hermetic quest, which is presented in the Corpus Hermeticum as a path upward through seven stages of the "cosmic framework," each of which purifies and advances adepts until "they rise up to the father in order and surrender themselves to the powers, and, having become powers, they enter into god. This is the final good for those who have received knowledge: to be made god."[45]

Avicenna's cosmology followed the emanationist scheme of celestial spheres in which our sublunar world represented the far end of the universe from its source. The "Active Intellect" or master of the sublunar world, transmitting emanations that came from Allāh through the celestial spheres, was understood to be Gabriel, the angel of revelation. Avicenna does not imagine Muḥammad as an ancient astronaut, and places emphasis on the journey's allegorical nature: "The journey was intellectual. He went by thought."[46] Avicenna's conception of the ascent through the spheres, even if disembodied, remained grounded in an understanding of how the physical universe was ordered. While Avicenna and other Muslim philosophers such as al-Farābī remained skeptical of astrologers' ambitions to predict the future and contributed toward a definitive separation of astrology from mathematical astronomy, they also accepted the view that celestial movements impacted earthly events, including human actions. In Avicenna's philosophical circles, this virtually went without saying. Calling Avicenna a Ṣūfī would be tricky, but the philosopher certainly theorized prophetology and mystical experience in ways that later Ṣūfīs would find useful.

Mystically inclined thinkers continued to read Muḥammad's

ascension through traditional cosmologies and the intersection of these sources in Muslim philosophical literature. Mystical theologian and "Seal of the Muḥammadan Saints," Ibn al-'Arabī, associated each of the seven days of the week with one of the seven planets and a specific prophet; on each day, the spiritual seeker could access from that day's prophet, in accordance with that prophet's particular station. On Sunday, for example, the seeker could learn from the prophet Idrīs/Enoch, who was associated with the Sun. As the Sun was the most central of the seven "planets" beyond the earth, Idrīs would reveal secrets that demonstrated his own position as a mystical pole or axis *(quṭb)*. The prophet Adam, as the original man, represented the Moon, since the Moon occupied a liminal state between the earth and the heavens, and transmitted emanations from the higher spheres into our earthly or sublunar realm.[47] The heavens were *the heavens*, without modern distinctions of "heavens" as conceived in separate scientific or religious contexts. Ibn al-'Arabī's articulations of unseen saintly hierarchies drew from medieval science: there were seven geographical districts of the earth, and each of these districts was guarded by one of seven saintly *'abdāl*; each of these 'abdāl received powers from the emanations of the seven planetary spheres, along with the prophets associated with those spheres.[48] There's no "science vs. religion" here; astronomy is part of the path.

For many readers today, living in a world in which science and religion are often (not always) understood to rule over separate territories of knowledge, the details of the ascension have departed from science to become purely *religious* facts. The ascension has not been rewritten for modern notions of a "solar system," in which the earth is one of eight or nine planets that revolve around an average-size star in an unimaginably minor neighborhood within a *universe*; nor have the discoveries of Uranus (1781), Neptune (1846), and Pluto (1930) caused major shake-ups to traditional cosmologies or resulted in new planetary esotericism. Nonetheless, even without changes to the traditional accounts, the ascension has been transformed. The notion of specific planets' associations with celestial spheres is forgotten, the entire physical universe can be reconceived as the first heaven, and Allāh's throne remains "up there" above everything, but today's meanings of "up there" would have been unimaginable to our predecessors.

Children of Abraham, Children of Saturn

An attempt to examine the question of "astrology in Islam" might first ask if Muslims are doing anything unique: If there is in fact an "Islamic position on astrology," is this position especially Islamic for any reason other than the sources cited and authorities to which one appeals? Can something be gained by carving all Muslim responses to astrology from their respective contexts and isolating them within the category of *Islam*? Does this actually paint a helpful picture of anything? Or does the category show its incoherence and start to disintegrate before our eyes?

Though now closer to the "magic" section of the bookstore, astrology once enjoyed the full prestige of science, and the assumptions upon which astrological traditions rested were widely accepted—even by astrology's most vehement opponents—as basic facts of nature. At another point in history, everyone knew that the earth occupied the center of a series of spheres, that these planets were embedded in the spheres, and that in our own sublunar realm, we were subject to the effects of forces moving in those spheres. Because there were seven planets—according to a definition of "planet" that included the Sun and Moon, but not the earth—there were seven celestial spheres, all existing within an outermost sphere that encompassed everything. Depending on one's precise religious orientation, these facts produced different consequences. But the consequences are too varied for us to name the "Islamic position" on astrology. Even if a Muslim accepted as valid the prophetic statements that prohibited the knowledge of stars as a form of detestable siḥr, this acceptance could still signify different openings and closures to different readers. Some Muslims regarded astrology as a kind of polytheism; others believed that astrology provided special evidence of harmony between heavens and earth that served to prove divine unity, the uncontested sovereignty of a shared creator and lord. There were even claims that astrological analyses of history proved Muḥammad's prophethood. Some Muslims acknowledged astrology's potential efficacy, but rejected the field as having originated via humans learning from jinns or demons. Their fellow Muslims, however, could cite alternate sources that repositioned astrology as having originated with genuine prophets who received this knowledge as divine revelation. And while the Qur'ān makes several references to stars without ever giving a clear verdict on the issue of astrology, both astrology's opponents and its supporters have cited the Qur'ān in support of their opinions.

While theologically driven opposition to astrology can be found in any period of Muslim history, believers who engage astrology today are likely to be accused not only of bad religion, but also of bad science. Astrology has surrendered its scientific gravitas, but believers continue to argue that science is on the side of their faith. Muslims disseminate pamphlets and Web sites attempting to prove that the Qur'ān contains miraculously advanced scientific knowledge regarding matters such as fetal development and geology. Christian opponents of evolution do not only counter Darwin with a valorization of blind faith in scripture, but have produced a sizable industry of textbooks, films, and even museums that claim to *scientifically* prove their scriptural creation narrative. Beyond natural sciences, religious adherents will play by the rules of dominant knowledge regimes even when attempting to refute them. So apologists for patriarchal norms might counter feminism by using arguments that only feminists made possible, i.e., defending conservative gender restrictions as *empowering* and *liberating* for the individual woman of faith against sexism and objectification that exist in broader society. Neotraditionalists can disdain modern critical theory but might pick up enough of it to wield against their opponents, without ever turning that tool upon their own assumptions about the "classical tradition" that they claim to know and represent.

The various rises and falls of astrology throughout history point to the instability of religions that we imagine as timeless and unchanging. In some historical settings, astrology provided a useful resource for proving one's own religious claims against whoever one marked as unbelievers, or clearly establishing God's favor for one empire against another. Different fields and methods have supplanted that resource, and I wonder if any tradition can survive these seismic shifts and remain the same tradition. Modern believers in any premodern tradition conceptualize the universe in ways that would have been unthinkable to their predecessors. Our ideas about the structure of created existence would make no sense to our coreligionists from previous eras, and perhaps not even to foundational and prophetic figures of the traditions that we claim. Is it the same Islam? Does Muḥammad's celestial ascension through the seven heavens preserve its "traditional" meanings and consequences if we no longer uphold these seven heavens as the actual organization of the universe? And what are the consequences as *we* claim the authority over our traditions to decide when premodern theologians, philosophers, mystics, or jurists speak only within the limits of their own world's science, as opposed to their universal and timeless truths?

If a consideration of Muslim astrologies throughout history points to the instability of Islam as a construct, it also challenges Islam's pristine purity and self-containment against other traditions. Astrology was a shared technology that crossed boundaries of faith confessions. Muslims, Christians, and Jews were doing similar things with the stars and actively informed each other's projects. This is in part because they shared similar conceptions of how the universe was ordered—and not only because they were all "children of Abraham," but perhaps more so because they studied the same corpus of scientific works, much of which was written by polytheists, and ascribed to shared sets of assumptions within their historical settings. Theophilus of Edessa (d. 785), a Christian who worked as court astrologer for the 'Abbāsid caliph al-Mahdī, calculated that Islam was to last 960 years, the amount of time that it would take for the Saturn-Jupiter conjunction to reappear in Scorpio.[49] In the early twelfth century, a Jewish astrologer in Spain calculated that in the year 1226, a great Saturn-Jupiter conjunction in Aquarius would correspond to the disappearance of both Christianity and Islam from the earth and herald the appearance of the Jewish Messiah.[50] His work relied on a tradition of conjunction-based prediction astrology that had been championed in Muslim caliphates, with its formative thinkers in the 'Abbāsid era being the Jewish astrologer Mashā'allāh and al-Kindī's Muslim/atheist disciple, Abū Ma'shar, who themselves worked with a pre-Islamic Persian legacy of reading kingdoms' rises and falls through Saturn-Jupiter conjunction theory.[51]

Because we are products of our own historical moment, Muslim beliefs today sometimes have more in common with the views of contemporary adherents of other religions (or even secular humanists!) than with Muslims from other periods. For those who mark consistency as a religion's first claim to legitimacy, this could be unsettling. To consider a field such as astrology and recognize its changes throughout Muslim traditions subjects Islam itself (along with the traditions imagined as Islam's "Abrahamic" cousin faiths) to the possibility of change. Meanwhile, taking a close look at Islamic astrology as a concept reveals Islam to be continually remade in collaboration with other traditions, denying the suggestion of a clear and stable "inside" that can ever hope for protection from the "outside."

5

Finding Hermes in the Qur'ān: The High Station of Idrīs

And we raised him to a high station.

—QUR'ĀN 19:57

In many traditions, we encounter believers who claim to live by the words of their sacred texts alone. This is not simply an anti-modern throwback to ancient literalism, as some critics would charge: it's in fact a thoroughly modern phenomenon, brought on by modern factors such as the domination of European Protestant empires, the new accessibility of scriptures through modern printing, and changing relationships between scripture and science. Scripturalism has flourished as a symptom of the modern individual, an autonomous reader with rising confidence that s/he could personally interpret the divine words for his/her own self, without the mediation of clerical authorities. Scriptural fundamentalism is not simply a reversion to old modes of knowledge:

the promise that scripture gives you a direct, personal encounter between the scripture's transcendent source and yourself is a modern response as much as anything, even when it claims to rescue us from modern ailments. It violates the same border between "modernity" and "tradition" that it constructs.

The claim to textual purity remains delicate, since the reader can only understand a scripture through countless referents that exist outside the scripture. The Qur'ān constantly speaks of people, places, and events with an assumption that we already know about them and can fill in the missing details for ourselves, which renders a truly "Qur'ān-only" Islam impossible. A scripture cannot shield its community from outside pollution when every word becomes an open window. With this in mind, it becomes less reflective of Islam in real life to argue over the meanings of the Qur'ān's words, since the Qur'ān itself could be less of a determining force than the various outside forces that act upon it. The borders separating a book's insides from what's outside are as flimsy and permeable as those dividing nations. No matter how many concrete walls, security fences, razor-wire coils, and surveillance towers a scripture's guardians set up to police its borders, there are always points of entry and exit—holes in the fence, tunnels underground—that expose the border as an illusion.

For numerous practitioners of sciences that some Muslim authorities would regard as illicit or demonic, such as astrology and geomancy, the Qur'ān's brief mentions of a prophet named Idrīs provided a valuable resource. Reading the character of Idrīs through a complex matrix of references, they were able to conceptualize their technologies as having been revealed by Allāh and taught to humankind through righteous prophets. The handful of Qur'ānic verses that refer to Idrīs, while providing almost no data on his life or prophetic mission, created a portal through which vast bodies of knowledge could pass into each other.

As with just about everything, the story begins in Egypt.

Divine Messengers and Prophet-Gods: Thoth and Hermes

Greek and Roman thinkers recognized in Egypt a culture older than their own, and with deeper archives; it was popularly believed in the Mediterranean milieu that Egyptians were the first to practice the systematized rituals that might be described in modern vocabulary as "organized religion."[1] Herodotus reports that when Hecataeus boasted to Egyptian priests that he could trace his lineage through 16 generations, the priests shut down his Hellenic pride by displaying their superior lineages, which went back 345 generations.[2] Neoplatonist philosopher Iamblichus (d. ca. 325 CE) believed that Egypt was the source of Greek philosophy, as figures such as Pythagoras had studied under Egyptian sages; he thus argued that because Egyptian prophets had been the first to achieve contact with the gods, their language worked better than Greek for performing effective rituals.[3] Similar to the premodern Orientalism with which Greeks alternately exoticized, fetishized, mocked, and feared Persian traditions—the historical process from which we get our word "magic"—Greeks and Romans viewed Egypt with awe for its alien knowledge and superior antiquity.

Greco-Roman fascination with Egyptian traditions seems to parallel modern Western fantasies of India or Tibet as "lands of spirituality," and would have been no more sophisticated. "Men of these less ancient nations were prepared to admire quite uncritically the temples and rituals of the Egyptians," writes Garth Fowden, "and even to accept the idea that the land of Egypt was intrinsically holy."[4] With Egypt so exceptionally well branded as a source of transcendent wisdom, Greek and Roman writers sometimes sought to authorize themselves with Egypt's prestige, often presenting their own works as having been revealed by Egyptian gods. These works, presented as supernatural revelations from exotic and foreign deities, mark the start of European Hermetic tradition. Examining this corpus, modern sensibilities would distinguish between works of philosophical or theological matters and those dealing with astrology or alchemy; as Fabrizio Lelli has argued, however, such a separation of categories reflects our own assumptions more than the authors' own views of how the universe worked.[5]

Central to the Greek appropriation of Egyptian wisdom traditions was the Egyptian god Djehuty, popularly represented in the form of a baboon, ibis, or ibis-headed man, and better known today by his Hellenized name, Thoth. Having invented hieroglyphics, Thoth was a god of writing and education, and was venerated as a patron god for various sciences. He served as the scribe of the gods, author of priestly ritual, and an attendant of Osiris. For his privileged access to the transcendent knowledge of the gods and association with human education and technology, Thoth was seen as a mediator between divine and human realms, a point of contact through whom humans could potentially obtain divine secrets. As the source of Egyptian religion, Greek thinkers latched onto Thoth, but also rewrote him in their terms. Greeks recognized Thoth as the Egyptian equivalent of Hermes, their own intermediary between divine and human realms. As Thoth was designated "twice great" and later "thrice great," the combined Thoth-Hermes became "thrice great," or Trimegistus.[6] Precise relationships between Hermes and Thoth, Hermes and Mercury, or Hermes and Hermes Trimegistus varied from one source to another. Egyptian priest Manetho identified Thoth as the first Hermes, who preserved knowledge in hieroglyphics to be retrieved after the Flood and then translated into Greek by the second Hermes.[7]

Unlike Thoth, who could transmit divine revelations to humanity but remained securely on the god side of the god-human division, Hermes was sometimes represented as a human who ascended to god status, rising after his death to become the planet Mercury. As a prophet-turned-god, Hermes came to signify the pinnacle of human spiritual perfection. Adepts who sought to transcend their earthly existence and achieve their own celestial ascensions appealed to Hermes for guidance. In Greek papyri, magical spells—or *prayers*?—beseech Hermes to visit devotees in their dreams and reveal secrets.[8]

Greek Hermeticists' boasts of Egyptian sources should not be accepted uncritically. The relationship of Greek Hermeticism to Egyptian religion could be analogous to Euro-American constructions of yoga versus South Asian yoga traditions: just as the representation of "timeless Indian tradition" at a commercial yoga center in New York could very well amount to nineteenth-century European gymnastics rebranded with Sanskrit terminology, we need to recognize Greek Hermeticism as appropriating, creatively reconstructing, and sometimes outright fabricating Egyptian tradition rather than simply transmitting it as is.

From this investment in Hermes as a source of celestial wisdom emerged a body of literature attributed to him, the *Corpus*

Hermeticum, expounding upon various fields of knowledge that would be termed "magical" or "occult" in today's terms. But the corpus also expresses a philosophical dimension to these fields, presenting their practices as a path of self-purification and perfection leading to knowledge of the divine and self:

> Thus, unless you make yourself equal to god, you cannot understand god; like is understood by like. Make yourself grow to immeasurable immensity, outleap all body, outstrip all time, become eternity and you will understand god. Having conceived that nothing is impossible to you, consider yourself immortal and able to understand everything, all art, all learning, the temper of every living thing. Go higher than every height and lower than every depth. Collect in yourself all the sensations of what has been made, of fire and water, dry and wet; be everywhere at once, on land, in the sea, in heaven; be not yet born, be in the womb, be young, old, dead, beyond death. And when you have understood all these at once—times, places, things, qualities, quantities—then you can understand god.[9]

Hermeticism, if we look closely enough at what's happening in its texts, betrays the magic-religion divide. In his various representations, Hermes appears as both a magus and a prophet; he is a god taught by angels; he is a human who teaches the deities Isis and Osiris; he offers astrology as a path of human perfection that leads toward knowledge of (and a degree of union and self-identification with) the One. If Solomon is a prophet who does the work of a sorcerer, Hermes reads like a sorcerer who also works as a prophet. Between these liminal figures, what separates their vocations? "Astrology, magic, and alchemy were included in the Hermetica," writes Florian Ebeling, "for they had a common theological-philosophical basis: the unity of the spiritual-divine had left its imprint on the multiplicity of earthly phenomena, with the result that all phenomena in the divine and earthly spheres were connected to one another."[10] As much as religion itself is a historically unstable domain, deciding that Hermeticism constitutes a field of knowledge separate from religion in any meaningful way remains untenable. In antiquity, the Hermetic model of prophethood or angelhood—or even godhood—was not so far removed from other models that Hermes could not be rewritten in their terms.

The Jewish Hermes: Enoch/Metatron

In an ancient urban center as diverse as Alexandria, Greek thinkers were not alone in their appropriation of Egyptian gods. Among Jewish communities in Alexandria that had elevated Moses to god status, some specifically identified Moses as Thoth/Hermes. The connection could have been intuitive: like Thoth/Hermes, Moses served as a legislator, a mediator through whom divine scripture could be revealed to humanity, and arguably as an innovator in written language, being the first person described in the Hebrew Bible as performing the task of writing.[11] Directly informed by Hecataeus's writings on Hermes as scribe of Osiris, namer of unnamed things, inventor of the alphabet, creator of music, and even the first to establish a wrestling school, Jewish writer Artapanus reproduces Moses as a thoroughly Thoth/Hermes-styled ascended master and culture-bringer.[12] Artapanus attributes to Moses the invention of various technologies, development of the hieroglyphs, establishment of circumcision for Egyptians and Ethiopians, and also the division of Egypt into thirty-six districts. In Artapanus's treatment, Moses becomes the origin for everything meaningful or noteworthy in Egyptian culture; Moses's introduction of boats and new methods of construction with stones to Egypt even made the pyramids possible.[13] As Herodotus, Plato, and Hecataeus had claimed that philosophy had originated in Egypt, Artapanus asserts that Egypt had first learned it from Moses, privileging Yahwist revelation as philosophy's true source.[14]

Artapanus also credits Moses with founding Egyptian religion, assigning districts to specific priests, deciding the gods that would be worshipped in each district, and determining the religious significance of animals such as cats, dogs, ibises, and other birds. While this may seem unbecoming of a prophetic Hebrew monotheist, the narrative of Moses teaching Egyptians their religion supports Artapanus's polemical point of Moses as singlehandedly bringing civilization to Egypt and structuring the entire society.[15]

Aramaic incantation bowls from late antique Iraq, expressing Jewish appeals for protection against a variety of sorceries and the evil arts of fallen angels, provide evidence that at least some practitioners equated Hermes with Metatron, a mysterious celestial being whose literary portrayal alternates between that of an angelified man and a semi-divine "lesser YHWH."[16] Nathaniel Deutsch argues that in his capacity as high priest in heaven, Metatron represents a nexus of the temple-centered religiosity that characterized the ancient Near East—redirected in Jewish thought after the destruction of the Temple in 70 CE toward imaginaries of a loftier temple high above the world—and the growing importance of "divine men" in late antiquity.[17] In addition to his imprecise human-angel-god status, Metatron shares some vocational overlaps with Hermes. Like Hermes, Metatron acts as a *psychopompos*, a guide who leads souls to the afterlife. Metatron also boasts privileged knowledge, claiming that "all mysteries of the Torah and all secrets of wisdom, and all depths of purity, and all thoughts of the hearts of living creatures, and all secrets of the world, and all the secrets of Creation are revealed before me as they are revealed before the Creator."[18] In further resonance with Hermes/Thoth, Metatron works as Yahweh's scribe and messenger.

Metatron corresponds to Hermes as a human who ascended to higher realms of knowledge and being. Traditions identify Metatron in his pre-angelic life as the prophet Enoch, inspired in part by Genesis 5:24: "Enoch walked with God; then he was no more, for God took him."[19] The Books of Enoch add depth and detail. Enoch is depicted as ascending through the seven heavens, witnessing the marvels of each, until reaching God's throne room. Losing his consciousness, Enoch is supported by Gabriel and then escorted by Michael before God, where he is stripped, anointed, and transformed into "one of the glorious ones." God assigns an angel to spend thirty days initiating Enoch into the celestial archive and its various knowledges. Upon completing his instruction, Enoch returns to the world and spends thirty days teaching what he had learned before his final ascension.[20]

The literary genre of the ascension narrative, as demonstrated in scholarship on Muḥammad's own journey through the heavens, offers a potent tool for authorizing mystics, adepts, sorcerers, and prophets, while marginalizing or discrediting rival claims. For Enoch's journey into the heavens and metamorphosis into an angel, Enochic literature identifies him as the Son of Man; it has been argued that this move served an anti-Christian polemic, countering Christian uses of the "Son of Man" title and positioning Enoch over Jesus as the true Son of Man and celestial god-prophet.[21] The transformation of Enoch into Metatron became a resource for both mystics and their opponents. For mystically inclined readers, the story of an advanced seeker ascending into the heavens and morphing into an angel or even demiurge provided an example of human perfection that at least theoretically remained achievable for all seekers. For authorities who were uneasy with mysticism, however, as well as the possible transgressions of God's supreme sovereignty in these depictions of the semi-divine celestial scribe and high priest, the character of Metatron was rewritten to discourage mystics from attempting to follow Enoch's path. Within rabbinic and Hekhalot literatures, we find an ascended master mistaking the angel-priest for a god, thus producing a cautionary tale on the dangers of mysticism.[22]

For his connection to the disclosure of divine knowledge and wisdom, Enoch/Metatron became associated with technologies by which other humans could attain celestial secrets, such as astrology. Having been trained by angels in the laws of stars and other celestial bodies, Enoch shares his knowledge with humankind and thus becomes the first teacher of astrology. This narrative legitimizes astrology as part of prophetic tradition and also demonstrates why, as Esther J. Hamori explains, "Recent scholarship has recognized that the long-assumed dichotomy between 'prophecy' and 'divination' is polemical, outdated, and not to be accepted as objectively factual any more than the emic presentations of 'religion' and 'magic' more broadly."[23] Enoch becomes a point of evidence in the deconstruction of that binary. However, the intersection of offices comes with a pious disclaimer: as a rightly guided prophet/angel, Enoch's use of these sciences conforms to permissions and instructions from God. While treating astrology as a true knowledge rooted in divine power, Enochic literature also demonizes illicit astrology as having been transmitted by fallen rebellious angels to their human followers.

Enoch operates as a hub of cultural exchange, moving not only between categories of knowledge but also between sources both east and west of Palestine: while Hellenized readers might have noticed parallels between Enoch and Hermes, the genealogy of Enoch's story reaches back to Mesopotamian scribal traditions. Scholars seeking to trace Enoch's textual DNA have connected him to the Babylonian figure of Enmeduranki. Genesis names Enoch as the seventh patriarch from Adam; Enmeduranki appears as the seventh ruler in various Mesopotamian king lists. Enmeduranki ruled as king of Sippar, the city-state that claimed association with sun god Shamash; Genesis assigns Enoch a life span of 365 years, linking him to the solar calendar. Like Enoch, Enmeduranki was a prophet who experienced a heavenly ascension, which included initiation into divine revelation and physical metamorphosis into a new angelic or semi-divine body.[24] In his celestial posthuman role, Enmeduranki employed divinatory methods to properly decode and interpret signs and unveil secret knowledge, which he then revealed to humans on behalf of the gods.[25]

All signs clearly point to Enoch as a literary character conforming to tropes of the Enmeduranki story; but the production of Enoch doesn't stop there. As textual resources and traditions flowed between Persia, Mesopotamia, Egypt, Palestine, Greece, and Rome, Enoch traveled between various characters, literatures, and meanings. At whatever arbitrary border divides two cultures or bodies of knowledge, we can often find an Enoch-shaped hole in the fence. When Muslim intellectuals believed that they had located references to Enoch within the Qur'ān, yet another portal opened. The naming of Enoch as a Qur'ānic prophet would also contribute toward identification of the Qur'ān's Enoch with Hermes, forming an Enochic-Qur'ānic-Hermetic triangulation that enabled bodies of literature to leak into each other.

Ibis-Headed Prophets

The Qur'ān's narrative of history presents an ongoing effort by the Creator to speak to humanity, using angelic and human intermediaries. According to the Qur'ān, every nation had received divine instruction through Allāh's appointed prophets. In the ḥadīth literatures, the global total of prophets runs as high as 124,000. The Qur'ān only names a hair more than two dozen of these prophets, most of whom are familiar through biblical traditions: Adam, Noah, Abraham and his sons, Moses, Jesus, and so on.

One of the less familiar prophets was Idrīs. At first glance, his name appears traceable to the Arabic *d-r-s* root, which carries meanings associated with study and teaching (these also happen to be the root letters of *madrāsa*, "school"), and premodern commentators considered this relationship. Other than a name, the Qur'ān tells us essentially nothing about Idrīs beyond calling him a truthful man and prophet (19:56) and one of the patient along with Ishmael and Isaac (21:85). However, the Qur'ān creates an opening with its cryptic and potentially provocative statement, "We raised him to a high station" (19:57). The precise nature of this "high station" is left unexplained, but silence and ambiguity opened the words to a multitude of possibilities, depending on the readers' own frames of reference.

For those who approached the Qur'ān with a background in biblical literature and the genre of ascension narratives, God's raising of Idrīs to a "high station" resonated with the aforementioned mystery of Enoch in Genesis 5:24: that Enoch "was no more, for God took him." It seems that fairly early in Islam's textual history, Muslims identified the Qur'ānic character of Idrīs and the biblical Enoch as one and the same prophet, which instantly provided interpreters of the Qur'ān with a backstory for this mysterious character. Identification as Enoch served to link Idrīs not only to the Bible, but to the variety of apocalyptic literatures that circulated among Jews, Christians, Manichaeans, and other communities in the Near East of late antiquity, in which Enoch featured prominently. Metatron would also find a home in Muslim literatures that modern scholars have designated as both magical and nonmagical,[26] his name appearing in philosophical works, in incantations attributed to the great philosopher/astrologer al-Kindī, on Shī'ī amulets, and in sorcerers' encyclopedias as well as Qur'ānically driven invocations.[27] Steve Wasserstrom describes Metatron as enjoying a "marketplace popularity" in Muslim Egypt, as demonstrated by his recurring appearances in thirteenth- and fourteenth-century magical collections.[28] In a departure from Jewish Merkaba literature that identified Metatron as Enoch, however, Muslim thinkers preferred to conceptualize

Metatron as Moses's mysterious teacher Khiḍr (an ambiguously human or angelic figure) or in explicitly angelic terms, a divine scribe at the right side of God's throne, sometimes equated with other named angels. Suyūtī describes Metatron (Mitatrush) as the angel "in charge of the veils," the only one who knows what lies beyond the "deserts of light" above the seventh heaven.[29] At least one text identifies Metatron as a jinn.[30] Though Metatron had a career of his own in Muslim literatures, it was one clearly separate from that of Enoch.

The Qur'ān's bare mention of Idrīs, supplemented with Enoch traditions, exploded with boundless capacity for producing meaning. With Idrīs established as Enoch, the "high station" that Allāh granted to him was not a merely metaphorical description of lofty status or prestige, but a reference to his literal ascension into the heavens, with possible implications of angelic instruction or even the taking of angelic form himself. As the character of Enoch shared resonances with Hermes, the connection of Enoch to Idrīs in turn created a meaningful opening for Hermeticism. The character of Hermes was known to early Muslim intellectuals, as the formative centuries of Islam's textual corpus were indelibly marked by the 'Abbāsid caliphate's massive translation project that brought vast libraries of Greek, Indian, and Persian literatures into Muslim thought. In this context, thinkers would refer to Hermes alongside classical scientists and religious heroes: One of the caliph Ma'mūn's viziers praised his knowledge by declaring that if dinner conversation turned to medicine, Ma'mūn was like Galen; if the topic was religion, Ma'mūn was like 'Alī; and if they discussed astrology, Ma'mūn equaled Hermes.[31] As Enochic and Hermetic literatures circulated, resonances and overlaps that could be observed between Enoch and Hermes, and Idrīs and Enoch, naturally enabled imaginations of Idrīs in relation to Hermes.

The Mu'tāzilī thinker Jāhiz (776–869), writing barely a decade after the reign of Ma'mūn, mentioned the association of Idrīs with Hermes. Astrologer Abū Ma'shar (787–886) would write of Hermes as not one, but countless distinct sages, of which three were especially important. The first Hermes, Adam's grandson, was the prophet identified by Jews as Enoch and Muslims as Idrīs. This Hermes was the first astrologer, builder of the Egyptian pyramids, and founder of cities, and he constructed the temple of Akhmim to preserve his knowledge prior to the Flood. The second Hermes lived in Babylon, where he trained Pythagoras in philosophy and mathematics. The third Hermes lived in Egypt, taught Asclepius, wrote on alchemy, and built temples.[32] Other versions of the "three Hermes" narrative identify Thoth as the son of Idrīs.[33]

The Hermes/Idrīs/Enoch triangle shows up as evidence in the famous tenth-century debate between the "two Rāzīs," Abū Ḥātim al-Rāzī (d. ca. 934) and Abū Bakr al-Rāzī (d. 925). Abū Ḥātim was an Ismā'īlī preacher endeavoring to defend what he understood as true Islam against the man whom he called simply "the mulḥid" (translated as "heretic"), physician/philosopher Abū Bakr, who defined the philosophical life as "making oneself similar to God . . . to the extent possible for a human being."[34]

In his takedown of Abū Bakr, Abū Ḥātim devotes a section to the philosopher's argument that great intellects of the past, such as Euclid, Ptolemy, Hippocrates, and Galen, had arrived at their knowledge by reason alone, without any need for the knowledge of prophets, and that these rational scientists had made greater contributions to society than those who relied on divinely revealed scriptures. Abū Ḥātim mentions the example of Idrīs, first teacher of the principles of astronomy. According to Abū Ḥātim, Allāh brought Idrīs to the top of the mountain at the world's navel, where Idrīs met an angel who taught him astronomy. "Among philosophers, he is called Hermes," Abū Ḥātim notes; "but in the Qur'ān, he is called Idrīs. These two names are similar to other names such as Galenus and Aristoteles and others that end with an *s*. In other revealed books, he is known as Enoch."[35] For Abū Ḥātim, Idrīs's multiplicity of names, along with the similarity between names of ancient prophetic/apostolic figures and philosophers, suggests a greater affinity between them than Abū Bakr is willing to allow.[36] For Muslims confronted with anxieties (either their own or those of authorities over them) regarding the Islamic legitimacy of Greek philosophy or sciences such as astrology, connecting these intellectual traditions to Muslim prophets subsumed them within an Islamic rubric. Pythagoras is therefore depicted as a student of Solomon's school in Egypt, granting Pythagorean thought the credibility of prophetic instruction.[37]

Idrīs vouches not only for astrology, but also for other sciences subject to religious challenge. One tradition named him as the first teacher of divinely revealed geomancy. Muslim accounts produced a teaching lineage that connected North African Berber master geomancer Abū 'Abd Allāh Muḥammad ibn 'Uthmān al-Zanātī through multiple generations back to Khalaf al-Barbarī the Elder, who lived during the time of Muḥammad and studied the geomancy of Ṭumṭum al-Hindī, who had been taught geomancy directly by Idrīs—who in turn had learned it as revealed knowledge from the angel Gabriel.[38] Linking philosophers and ancient sages to prophets mentioned in the Qur'ān (and even the Qur'ān's own angelic mode of delivery) expanded the possibilities for both Muslim intellectuals and non-Muslims living under Muslim rule.

The Ṣābians of Ḥarrān

The historian al-Mas'ūdī (896–956), who considered Idrīs, Enoch, and Hermes to have been the same prophetic personage, credits a community in Ḥarrān with first identifying Idrīs as Hermes. By representing Hermeticism as guidance from a prophet who was named in the Qur'ān, the Ḥarrānians were able to present their doctrines and practices—described in contemporary scholarship as a creative assemblage of elements from Mesopotamian, Indian, Iranian, Syrian, and Greek religious, philosophical, and astrological/astronomical schools[39]—as qualifying for legal recognition by the caliphate. Claiming Hermes as Idrīs and their own local prophet supported a larger Ḥarrānian project of self-identifying with a mysterious group that the Qur'ān named as prophetically guided.

In its typology of religious difference, the Qur'ān mentions "Ṣābians" along with Christians, Jews, and Magians as communities between whom God will offer the final judgment (2:62, 5:69, 22:17). As opposed to polytheists, Jews and Christians were to be granted the rights of legally protected minorities under Muslim rulers (this "People of the Book" privilege was also extended to Zoroastrians, despite their more ambiguous status). Unlike Jews and Christians, who are frequently mentioned in the Qur'ān and chronicles of Muḥammad's life as participants in the early Muslim community, however, it does not appear that Muḥammad or his Companions ever encountered Ṣābians in person. Nor does the

Qur'ān give any description of where Ṣābians could be found or what exactly they believed; nor were Ṣābians referenced in any source contemporary to the Qur'ān.[40] The Qur'ān tells us that there are people called Ṣābians, and that Allāh approves of them; beyond that, Muslim thinkers were left with no concrete information on the community.

In its pre-Islamic life, Ḥarrān had been a city dedicated to the moon god Sin. As Sin delivered the gods' oracles and functioned as the lord of knowledge, the flat disc of the moon was imagined as a tablet on which divine decrees were written. The gods' scribe who wrote on the moon, Nabu (or Nebo), also happened to be the inventor of writing, patron of science, and the knower of human destinies, and was associated in Mesopotamian astral/planetary religion with Mercury; he would naturally be associated with Hermes, Thoth, Enoch/Idrīs, and other regional equivalents.[41] Ḥarrān was religiously heterogeneous, home to numerous communities and their traditions; it might have been a refuge for polytheist intellectuals amid the previous centuries' rise of imperial Christianity.

The city was subjected to theologically driven violence in the decades prior to Islam, as Stephen, Bishop of Ḥarrān, received orders in 590 CE from the Byzantine emperor to massacre polytheists who would not accept Christ. However, when Ḥarrān first came under Muslim rule by peaceful surrender in 639 or 640 CE, polytheists were still present and apparently the ones who negotiated with the Muslim conquerors.[42] Peace was interrupted by intra-Muslim strife, during which Ḥarrān was taken and retaken by rival factions. The Ḥarrānians sided with Mu'āwiya against 'Alī in the Battle of Siffin, for which 'Alī reportedly punished the city with mass slaughter.[43]

In addition to polytheists, Christians, Jews, and new Muslims, Ḥarrān was also home to a group that developed its own local system, a unique amalgamation of resources. They practiced Hermetic sciences such as astrology, worshipped celestial bodies in manners popular to the region, reportedly believed in reincarnation, and regarded their system as the oldest and most pure expression of divinely revealed truth. Above the door to their assembly hall, one encountered the inscription, "He who knows himself is deified" (*man 'arafa dhātahu ta'allaha*).[44] The group did not seem to have a name, nor did its eclectic incorporation of diverse materials easily play into the Muslims' categories. For Muslim rulers who differentiated between various non-Muslim communities based on a clear binary between guided groups (monotheistic, prophetically founded, possessing scripture) and the ignorant (polytheistic, no prophets, no scriptures), this Ḥarrānian community might have confused the modes of assessment.

Tenth-century scholar Ibn al-Nadīm gives an account ("that is, in all probability, untrue," writes Tamara M. Green, "but nonetheless instructive"[45]) of the 'Abbāsid caliph al-Ma'mūn visiting the city in 840 CE and quizzing locals as to their confessional identity, scripture, and prophet; when they cannot answer, al-Ma'mūn declares them unbelievers whose blood is lawful to shed. The Ḥarrānians answer that they will pay the poll tax, which al-Ma'mūn refuses; the poll tax is only accepted from communities that are mentioned in the Qur'ān, such as Christians and Jews, who have their own revelations and prophets. Al-Ma'mūn allows the Ḥarrānians a grace period to sort out their religion, during which they reportedly take a Muslim shaykh's advice to self-identify as Ṣābians, thus securing legal protection as a group sanctioned in the

Qur'ān.[46] The identification of Hermes with Idrīs likewise gave them a Qur'ānically endorsed prophet to call their own, while sanctifying Hermetic literature as their prophetically transmitted scripture.[47] Through this narrative, the self-identified Ṣābians of Ḥarrān sought to escape the stigma of polytheism and achieve recognized minority status alongside monotheist traditions.

Muslim intellectuals produced a variety of reactions to the Ḥarrānians' claimed identity, and even skeptical responses often engaged aspects of the Ḥarrānians' narratives as accepted history. Al-Birūnī believed that the Ṣābians of Ḥarrān could be traced back to Persian ruling elites in Balkh who worshipped celestial bodies and embraced the original Ṣābian religion, which was taught by Budhasaf (Buddha), whom some identified as Hermes.[48] Dimashqī does not accept the Ḥarrān Ṣābians' self-presentation as the Ṣābians of the Qur'ān, but believes that their name came from Ṣābi, son of Hermes—whom he identifies as Idrīs.[49] The seminal jurist Ibn Taymiyya mentions Ṣābians in his condemnation of astrology, though Yahya Michot notes that for Ibn Taymiyya, the term "Ṣābians" could refer to any star worshippers or idolaters, "ancient or otherwise, from Greece to China"; similarly, Ibn Taymiyya treats "Hermes" as a title in the manner of Caesar, rather than a personal name.[50] Describing Ṣābian astrological traditions as "darknesses piled on top of each other," Ibn Taymiyya ridicules astrology's practitioners as opposed to both religion and reason.[51] Especially infuriating to Ibn Taymiyya is the suggestion that Idrīs, a genuine prophet of Allāh, could be associated with astrology and even astrolatry. Ibn Taymiyya charges that no authentically transmitted reports link prophets to such illicit arts; these practitioners only make their case by referring to their "Hermes of the Hermeses, and they pretend that he is Idrīs."[52] The shaykh does allow, however, that astronomical knowledge for the purposes of computation constitutes a "valid science," and that it's not impossible for Idrīs to have been the first teacher of that science.[53]

The linkage of Idrīs to Hermes does not require a singular origin from which all future references would branch out. Once Idrīs and Enoch were linked, association with Hermeticism would seem intuitive for many readers. But if the Ḥarrān community had developed their narrative of the Idrīs-Hermes connection as part of a legal strategy, F. E. Peters notes "justice" in their move. In legitimizing their tradition by claiming to be the Ṣābians of the Qur'ān and rebranding Hermes as the prophet Idrīs, they repeated an earlier Hermetic process. After all, Greco-Roman writers had identified Hermes as Thoth to appropriate the prestige and credibility of Egyptian heritage for their own projects. "Just as Hermes-Thoth was used to conceal the true nature of the original philosophical-theosophical melange," Peters writes, "so now Idrīs was summoned to give Hermes a protective Islamic coloration by serving as a pseudepigraph for a pseudepigraph."[54]

The Ṣabians of Ḥarrān were not exactly "Muslims," since they claimed their right to legal recognition not as followers of Muḥammad, but as a non-Muslim community that the Qur'ān acknowledged with respect. Yet this meant that even as non-Muslims, they argued within the logic of Islam, authorizing themselves through the Qur'ān and claiming that their prophet, Hermes, was fully endorsed by the Qur'ān as Idrīs. To a reader with eyes directed by prevailing modern assumptions—in which religions are imagined as interacting with each other on a theoretically neutral field of "secular" public space—the Ṣābians of Ḥarrān might appear to have been at least publicly Muslim in the sense that they played by Islam's rules, authorizing their existence through the Qur'ān's vision of prophetic history. As such, they became important participants in Islam as an intellectual tradition, both drawing from it and contributing resources for its future thinkers. Their astral theology would circulate among Muslim philosophical currents in tenth-century Baghdad, alongside numerous other schools and sectarian groups that sought to establish themselves as authorities of Islam as well as heirs to the knowledge of pre-Islamic sages.[55]

The Ṣabians of Ḥarrān appear to have been particularly salient for the rise of the Ikhwān al-Ṣafā' ("Brothers of Purity"), an "esoteric fraternity of lettered urbanites" based primarily in Baṣra with a second branch in Baghdad.[56] Amid the various Muslim groups competing for authority in tenth-century Iraq, this secret brotherhood sought to restore "true" Islam through harmonization of revealed knowledge with the Greek philosophical heritage.[57] The end result of the Ikhwān's purification project led to a system that claimed justification from various ancient sources, ranging from Pythagoras to Muḥammad, incorporating Qur'ān interpretation and ḥadīth citations alongside astrally determined prophetic cycles, Saturn-Jupiter conjunction theories, and notions of sacred numbers, for which one scholar described the Ikhwān's approach as "a syncretism of syncretisms."[58] For their openness to eclectic use of Greek, Persian, and Indian traditions, and perhaps especially their clear Shī'ī (and likely *Ismā'īlī* Shī'ī) affiliation, the Ikhwān would have appeared as dangerous heretics and subversive agents for many Muslims in the era that saw Sunnī Islam's ongoing crystallization. Nonetheless, their writings and ideas traveled beyond the limitations of their brand, even informing the thought of Sunnīs who otherwise might have been their most vehement opponents.

The Ikhwān became known through the dissemination of their encyclopedia, the *Epistles of the Brothers of Purity*. The last of their fifty-two *Epistles*, devoted to siḥr, incantations, and the evil eye, provides discussions of Ṣabian initiation rituals, and is one of the *Epistles* to have entered into Latin translation and dissemination in Europe.[59] The Ikhwān's project of universalizing knowledge and synthesizing traditions, presenting the philosopher's path as a mystical quest beyond matter, finds some personification in the figure of Hermes, who appears in the *Epistles* and is identified with Idrīs/Enoch. The Ikhwān reads the Qur'ān's statement "We raised him to a high station" to mean that Idrīs/Enoch/Hermes ascended to the celestial sphere of Saturn and remained there for thirty years, during which he observed all states of that sphere. After this period of three decades studying Saturn's cycle, the prophet returned to earth and taught astrology to humankind.[60] That Idrīs/Enoch/Hermes could ascend into the heavens—without his body—provided the Ikhwān with a template of the perfected philosopher-sage that they could hope to imitate.[61]

Hermetic Ṣūfism

John Walbridge, leading academic authority on Suhrawārdī (d. 1191 CE), argues that we should see Suhrawārdī primarily as a philosopher, but allows that this does not mean "philosopher" in the modern sense of the term. "The whole notion that there is some distinction to be made among philosopher, mystic, and magician," he writes, would have been completely alien to Suhrawārdī, as also with Neoplatonists and other ancient philosophical schools.[62] To look at the importance of Hermes for Suhrawārdī's philosophical system doesn't require that we sort out philosophical, mystical, or magical Hermeticisms from each other.

Suhrawārdī was a mystical philosopher in that he used philosophy to systematize mystical modes of knowing, and mystical visions informed his philosophy. He could engage the great philosophers of the past not only through what survived of their teachings, but directly through mystical experience: a turning point in his career occurred when he received a dream visitation from Aristotle, who confessed to the supremacy of Plato but also praised ecstatic Ṣūfī mystics Manṣūr al-Ḥallāj and Abū Yāzid al-Bisṭāmī as the true philosophers.[63] When Suhrawārdī asked Aristotle about the nature of knowledge, Aristotle answered, "Return to yourself."[64]

Suhrāwārdī's Illuminationist (Ishrāqī) school conceptualized knowledge in terms of light, which reached humankind from the One (the Light of Lights) through a chain of lesser lights in an emanation scheme. The source of knowledge is ultimately divine light, provided through mediating lights, to which the human soul can open itself through a process of spiritual perfection. Those willing to embark on the Illuminationist project could conceivably become advanced knowers, joining the ranks of the Brothers of Abstraction (*ikhwān al-tajrīd*) and Masters of Vision (*ashāb al-mushāhada*). Among the greatest knowers, Suhrawārdī names Plato, Muḥammad, and Hermes.[65] Walbridge writes that of all these ancient sages who enter into Suhrawārdī's eclectic matrix of resources, "Hermes is the most prestigious."[66] Hermes, according to Suhrawārdī, was the true originator of the Illuminationist school; from Hermes's school in Egypt, the "science of illumination" (*ilm al-ishraq*) persisted in Greek genealogies through sages such as the Egypt-trained Pythagoras, Empedocles, and Plato, and in Persian traditions both through pre-Islamic priest-kings and the later Ṣūfism of al-Ḥallāj. Hermes/Idrīs occupies the Islamic office of prophet here, but also does much more, expanding Suhrawārdī's terrain far beyond any particular confession. The Hermetic narrative constructs Illuminationism as a global, universal system, expressing timeless truths that cannot be constrained to one revelation or transmitted tradition, and establishes Suhrawārdī's teachings as the perfect and complete reconciliation of the Hermetic branches.

Having designated himself as the restorer of this universal wisdom, was Suhrawārdī claiming a kind of prophethood or messianic authority? Existing clerical and state regimes were threatened by his self-presentation. He alienated Aleppo's conservative religious scholars (*'ulama*) in debate, and some might have interpreted his arguments as revealing an Ismā'īlī affiliation—a dangerous position in Saladin's vehemently anti-Shī'ī regime—or, even more problematic, the claim to a prophetic station. Suhrawārdī was reported to have told the 'ulama that Allāh could *theoretically* create a prophet after Muḥammad, if Allāh so desired; this would have not only sparked charges that Suhrawārdī had apostatized from Islam, but also provoked questions of whether Suhrawārdī wanted an opening for his own prophethood. Suhrawārdī additionally had a reputation for displaying his spiritual advancement through marvelous acts, such as producing a chicken-egg-sized ruby from nowhere.[67] Whether such demonstrations amounted to God-given saintly miracles, demonic arts, or fraudulent hocus-pocus, of course, might have depended on how one already felt about Suhrawārdī's teachings. At some point, for reasons that remain speculative, Suhrawārdī was executed at the age of thirty-seven and became known as al-Maqtūl, "the Murdered."

Suhrawārdī's Illuminationism survived after his execution and became significant for Muslim thought, notably in the case of Ṣūfī orders such as the Chistīyya, as well as Iranian philosophers. His teachings also appealed to non-Muslims. Zoroastrian thinkers were drawn to this Muslim thinker in part for his engagements of Zoroastrian angelology and praise of pre-Islamic Persian traditions, leading to the establishment of a Zoroastrian Illuminationist school among Persian diasporas in India.[68]

Muslim Hermes, Hermetic Qur'ān

Examining Suhrawārdī's praise of Hermes as "father of philosophers," Walbridge encourages contemplation of the strange process through which "an Egyptian god with a Greek name could have found a central place in the philosophical tradition of a religious community that prided itself on its utter rejection of paganism."[69] Hermes appears everywhere as an agent of deconstruction, continually taking on new identities to blend into his new surroundings and producing new categories that disintegrate categories altogether—what does a construction of "Muslim Hermeticism" do to our constructions of both Islam and Hermeticism? Or the oppositions between prophet and diviner, prophet and philosopher, theologian and astrologer, mystic and wizard, monotheism and polytheism, or dīn and siḥr? Magic was rooted in philosophical traditions, philosophy was divine revelation, and prophets knew the secrets of the stars. When an Egyptian/Greek god gets successfully rebranded as a Jewish/Muslim prophet or a "Christian before Christ" whose oracles foretold the coming of Jesus and whose image was painted on church walls in post-Byzantine Eastern Europe,[70] or one scholar uses the term "astral religion" and another uses "astral magic" to describe *the exact same assemblage of texts, beliefs, and rituals*, our vocabularies start to fail us.

The Qur'ān repeatedly argues against mistaking prophets for sorcerers, perhaps because the differences between one class and the other are not as obvious as some of us would like: the Qur'ān seeks to enforce an insecure isolation. Even Muḥammad potentially undermines the clarity of our divisions. Muḥammad soars in his own (Hermetic?) ascent, rising through the successive layers of heavens with an angelic escort, conversing with past prophets, passing initiatic tests, witnessing pleasures and torments of the afterlife, and returning to earth with divine instructions (the five daily prayers) as well as the credibility of an audience with Allāh. This presentation of Muḥammad as an ascended master seeks to authorize him in conformity to a popular literary genre of the ancient Near East, and one that is not entirely monotheistic in its heritage. When scholars dismiss "theosophical Ṣūfīs" as promoting Platonized theologies that transcended "Islam's Abrahamic horizons,"[71] I wonder where we might begin to locate those horizons. At what point in history can we observe an "Abrahamic theology" in its purest form, bearing no trace of mixture or interference from Greek or Persian intellectual traditions or various local systems and practices, if such encounter and exchange produced our notions of the "Abrahamic" in the first place? How do we examine the diversity of traditions that make claims on Abraham and choose one that allows us to decide the "pure" Abrahamic system? We would have a hard time finding transgressions from these "theosophical Ṣūfīs" that did not already exist *within* Abrahamic traditions prior to Ṣūfism or even Islam. It could be argued that the very concept of "Satan" emerged as a result of Jewish interactions with Zoroastrians during the Babylonian captivity, and that even belief in a personified Devil therefore *transcended Abrahamic horizons* as these horizons would have been defined in another time. There were also contexts in which "Abrahamic horizons" included representations of Abraham as a master astrologer, Solomon as a student of Pythagoras, Pythagoras as a student of Solomon, and Moses as the founder of Egyptian polytheism—not to mention Christ as a Hellenized man-god or Muḥammad's prophethood emerging within a setting characterized by diversity and hybridity. So where are the limits? If there is such a thing as an Abrahamic tradition, we have to recognize that this construction is not impermeable; Abrahamic tradition remains porous, with elements constantly moving in and out on every side.

It becomes less useful to speak of "syncretism" when leakage and blending represent the normal state of affairs, rather than a curious break in an otherwise stable separation of systems. Nor does the idea of a coherent, self-evident "orthodoxy" provide a relevant framework for thinking about anything other than shifting power relations. If Saladin had decided to follow Suhrāwārdī instead of ordering his execution, Suhrawārdī's Illuminationist school could have ended up with orthodox privilege, and "mainstream" Sunnī imaginations could have been changed forever, allowing new space for Aristotle dream visions and Zoroastrian angels to find inclusion *within* Abrahamic horizons.

The frailty of the system—or the illusion of a system—becomes highlighted when we look at the English translation of the Qur'ān by Muḥammad Taqi ud-Dīn al-Hilali and Muhsin

Khan. For some time now, the Hilali-Khan Qur'ān has enjoyed prestige as the translation favored by the Saudi government's media complex, which would brand it in the eyes of many readers as a safe and trustworthy bastion of timeless Islamic orthodoxy. In the translation's parenthetical notes, Idrīs is identified as Enoch. Today, recognizing Idrīs and Enoch as the same prophet is perfectly "orthodox" to such a degree that no one ever feels the need to explain it or dig deeper or historicize the process by which these characters became intertwined, let alone consider the new connections that are activated when we name one as the other. It is an assumed orthodoxy so thoroughly established that it can spit heresy in your face and you wouldn't notice. The same conservative scholars who police the edges of what they see as legitimate Islam, guarding against any sign of mingling with non-Islamic traditions, confidently bring Enoch into the Qur'ān's roster of prophets without concern for what he brings with him. And yet no one could imagine speaking of the official religious discourse of the Kingdom of Saudi Arabia as "syncretic." Time covers all syncretism, smoothing over the folds.

With Enoch finding shelter in the Qur'ān, and thus helping to bring the Qur'ān into conversation with a vast corpus of Enochic/Hermetic literatures and sciences, the final binary to be troubled by this shape-shifting prophet/angel/god is that fabricated division between the Qur'ān's *inside* and its *outside*. Across the board, this is how texts work with each other: Alexandrian Christians claimed Hermes as their own prophet because they assumed that the word *logos* in the Hermetica referred to Christ.[72] Scripturalists who claim that the Qur'ān alone contains all of the answers do not recognize the sounds of their own voices. When the Qur'ān refers to something called siḥr or a prophet named Idrīs, it immediately reaches outside itself, relying on its readers' prior knowledge to fill in the blanks. In this same movement, the Qur'ān pulls outside resources into its words in order for the words to mean anything at all. The textual "fundamentalists" aren't wrong in their charges of mixture and corruption, but if they really followed their own critique, their whole world would collapse.

6

Your 1/46th Share of Prophecy: Dreaming Muḥammad

I heard my father say, "The Lord of Glory appeared to me in a dream and I asked him how best to draw nearer to him. 'Through my speech, Aḥmad,' he said. 'Do we have to understand it?' I asked. He said, 'It works whether you understand it or not.'"

—'ABD ALLĀH IBN AḤMAD IBN ḤANBAL, IN IBN AL-JAWZĪ'S *Virtues of the Imām Aḥmad ibn Ḥanbal*[1]

Some two decades before the time of this writing, I decided that intellectual disillusionments and confusions had overtaken my faith to such a degree that I could no longer call myself a Muslim. Heartbroken, I left a box of prayer rugs and ḥadīth collections outside the local mosque for whoever wanted them, and even disposed of my Qur'āns. One night amid this period of intensifying estrangement from Islam, I experienced a dream in which four men surrounded and embraced me, shielding me within their warm tangle of arms. Though I could not see their faces, I knew *exactly* who they were: Muḥammad, his son-in-law 'Alī, and grandsons Ḥasan and Ḥusayn. Comforted by these transcendent heroes, I knew that I was going to be okay, that I was loved and would remain loved no matter what name I gave to my religion. Wherever my journey might have taken me in relation to religious law and community, I was a Muslim with Muḥammad in my heart, or at least a version of him.

The paradox of the dream was that it affirmed me as a Muslim even as I imagined myself to be leaving Islam, presenting my acts of apostasy as somehow blessed by the Prophet and his family. Even as I emptied my house of Qur'āns—sometimes in regrettably disrespectful fashion—our dream embrace prevented the break from becoming absolute. In the imaginal dream world, beyond success or failure with checklists of correct *'aqīda* (dogma) points, I retained my connection to the Prophet. The dream allowed me to leave without ever being *gone*, and to stay without being trapped; by blessing my attempted apostasy, it made full apostasy impossible.

Many years later, I experienced a visionary encounter not through nighttime dreaming but rather through ayahuasca, the psychoactive Amazonian tea that has grown popular north of the equator in various spiritual and medicinal contexts. During my ayahuasca experience, I encountered the woman who was missing from my dream of the four men: Fāṭima, the daughter of Muḥammad, wife of 'Alī, and mother of Ḥasan and Ḥusayn. After several hours, the vision ran its course, and I ventured to the mosque. Though the vision's content included elements that would be considered theologically dangerous or even unspeakably blasphemous, it landed me back in a fully "orthodox" Sunnī setting, joining my sisters and brothers in regular prayer.

In my own life as a Muslim, dreams and drug visions have served to undermine the notion that I had to be either *in* or *out* of Islam, because the visionary experiences that would ostensibly throw me out also built bridges and healed wounds between the mosque and myself.

Where in our bag of categories—religious, "spiritual but not religious," magical, esoteric, occult—should we place our dreams? In today's bookstores, volumes on dream interpretation often find homes on the shelves next to books on reincarnation, the power of positive thinking, astrology, and tarot (within a section that might be located *near* the religion section, but nonetheless remains a separate entity—or perhaps a shared "religion/spirituality" bookcase). Medieval bookshelves would have been organized by different terms. Classical Muslim thinkers produced an immense body of literature devoted to *ta'bīr*, the deciphering of dreams, much of it resting comfortably within sharī'a-centered Sunnī and Shī'ī intellectual worlds. Though a closer look at Muslim literatures of dream interpretation, as with everything else in Muslim traditions, reveals the field to be less purely "Islamic" than a product of encounter and exchange with numerous sources and contexts, by no means was ta'bīr challenged as an illicit science in the manner of astrology or siḥr.

One of the classical Muslim terms for dream, *ru'yā*, literally means "vision" and also appears in discussions of mystical encounters experienced by the wakeful. My experience of ru'yā under the effects of ayahuasca would be more controversial than my visions of Muḥammad while asleep, since ayahuasca constitutes a deliberate chemical intervention as well as an obvious indulgence in other religious traditions. Of course, these judgments can be challenged by modern understandings of dreams and the historical reality of religious traditions as inescapably mixed from the start. Nonetheless, drugs are complicated. After the release of my Islam-and-ayahuasca book, *Tripping with Allah*, a Muslim reader wrote to me with interest in trying ayahuasca but asked whether such a practice constituted black magic. I did not know what to tell her, since these categories have lost most of their usefulness for me. Meanwhile, some reviewers described the book as a work of genuine mysticism.

Such responses to *Tripping with Allah* provoked questions for me of how we identify both magic and mysticism, and where one begins or the other ends. Reciting formulas to treat illness would appear to some as a magical practice; reciting formulas to invite dreams or visions of the Prophet sounds like a mystical discipline; but they could potentially switch labels. And where do you place someone who sees Muḥammad in a dream and is then cured of her ailment? When I drank ayahuasca and swallowed clay from the sacred desert of Karbala, mixing the two sacraments in my stomach, had I produced a *magical* potion to conjure spirits, or could this be called a *mystical* adventure? What would mark the difference—perhaps a fully systematized and articulated theology to define (and regulate) the chemical events in my bloodstream?

Many believers today are embarrassed by the notion of dreams as sources of religious content. Dreams can be incoherent, irrational, and ultimately destabilizing, while coherence, rationality, and consistency are popularly imagined as crucial fences that maintain the separation between religions of integrity and ignorant superstition. Religion in the modern world is often characterized by increasing pressures for believers to verify their faith by empirical methods—hence the popularity of evangelical Christian books, Web sites, and even museums that seek to prove the compatibility of modern science with literalist readings of the Bible. Muslims engage in their own versions of this project, insisting that the Qur'ān's divine authorship can be proven by revealing advanced scientific knowledge within the text. Many Muslim writers have claimed that the Qur'ān expresses scientifically verifiable truths that could not have been available in the seventh century CE. Though the Qur'ān doesn't actually offer any claims on human fetal development that would have been out of place in the seventh-century Mediterranean milieu (and reads as more or less compatible with Aristotle), Muslim pamphleteers frequently claim that the Qur'ān's embryology makes it impossible to deny the text as supernaturally revealed.

For many Sunnī Muslims, the truth-making power of modern scientific rationality resonates with a particular brand of neotraditionalism and revival of classical Muslim scholarship. These discourses emphasize the historical integrity of the ḥadīth corpus, the vast body of literatures depicting actions and sayings of Muḥammad, as a faithfully transmitted textual tradition and an archive with transcendent authority. The premodern scholars who preserved and promoted this tradition, we are told, were blessed with virtually superhuman memories and practiced impeccably critical rigor. They not only memorized immense archives of prophetic transmissions, but managed to identify and surgically extract the mistakes of less masterful scholars and even the fabrications and forgeries of liars.

This vision of "classical Islamic knowledge" presents a tradition that stands beyond argument: we are to place our trust in premodern scholars who were smarter than us and authorized by better teachers. They worked harder and for many more years than we ever could, and possessed not only superior intellectual rigor but also impeccable moral character and religious devotion. These scholars could also be regarded as mystics whose religious lives were greatly impacted by their dreams and transrational modes of knowledge, but such an image of the classical Muslim intellectual has limited usefulness today. The *modern* imagination of *traditional* Islamic learning consists primarily of students traveling to institutions in cities such as Cairo or Medina to sit at the feet of scholars and digest raw content, not dreamers and visionaries who receive transmissions from the unseen realm.

As contemporary American institutions such as Zaytuna College and AlMaghrib assert their qualifications to preserve and promote Islamic knowledge as a reliably transmitted textual tradition, they also tend to package the great scholars of the past in ways that will make the most sense to their audiences. This means that at an AlMaghrib seminar dedicated to the seminal traditionist Bukhārī on a university campus in Calgary, I was fed an image of Bukhārī that would resonate with the struggles and ambitions of modern university students. Bukhārī came off in the presentations as an ambitious alpha-nerd who was really, *really* great at school, loved his teachers, memorized mountains of data, aced every exam, and consistently outshone all of his peers. This depiction of the great scholar, while of course historically reasonable, did not prioritize possibilities for thinking about him as a mystic, though the ḥadīth master believed in ḥadīths that conceptualized dreams as 1/46th of prophecy and taught that seeing Muḥammad in a dream amounted to *really* seeing him. In other words, his scholarship affirmed nonscholarly modes of knowing.

Besides being the star student, Bukhārī was inspired to embark on his massive ḥadīth collection project by a dream in which he saw himself swatting flies away from Muḥammad's face. The dream signified to Bukhārī that he would purify Muḥammad's sublime custom, his Sunna, from fabricated sayings and actions that were falsely attributed to him. Bukhārī did not interpret the dream for insights into his own subconscious mind, but as a direct communication from Muḥammad. A similar dream was experienced by al-Ash'arī, the star theologian who left the rationalist Mu'tāzila movement to join the proto-Sunnī ḥadīth partisans and thereby made an enormous intellectual contribution to Sunnī tradition. Both of these men experienced their dream-visions more than two centuries after Muḥammad's death, but accepted it as a fact of nature that the Prophet was still capable of communicating with believers.

"Orthodox Islam" as many would recognize it today did not yet exist as such in the age of Bukhārī and al-Ash'arī; their scholarly and theological works played formative roles in producing and crystallizing what now bears the prestige of "orthodoxy" and "Sunnī tradition." In the centuries after them, a particular construction of Sunnī consciousness came to be branded as normative, mainstream, numerically dominant Islam, Islam as defined by a self-affirming corpus of seminal texts. This corpus does allow for dreams to be taken seriously, and by no means would it be considered radical or heretical to lean into dreams as a spiritual resource. But I am interested in the possibility of dreams and visions as a Deleuzian "line of flight," a means by which the structure of Sunnī intellectual tradition enables escape from itself. Dreams can disrupt and mutate textual knowledge, enable breaks from its authorities, produce new paths that had previously been unthinkable, provide "orthodox" routes to "heretical" destinations, and even restore us within the texts as something new. Dreams can open us to unknowing, rendering as once again mysterious what we now imagine as scientifically verified. Dreams can also open the Prophet; dreams open Muḥammad to no longer be read and interpreted as a historically bounded person acting within his own context, or even as a divinely authorized legislator or source of universal norms. In dreams, Muḥammad becomes exposed to our own world, and we are exposed to him: Muḥammad can speak directly to our own lives. For those of us struggling when the sacred sources and their deep entourages of supplementary literatures seem to fail us, dreams can affirm our attachments to the sacred sources from a place beyond them. Dreams can ease the distress in our points of unknowing; when the dead Muḥammad of books shuts us out, the living Muḥammad of our dreams can welcome us back in. For many of us, dreams provide our best or only chance.

Dreams, the Qur'ān, and Prophetic Sunna

Dreams are referenced in both the Qur'ān and the textual sources on Muḥammad's life and teachings. The Qur'ān acknowledges symbolic dream interpretation as a legitimate skill in its story of the prophet Yūsuf (Joseph). Biographies of Muḥammad, as well as ḥadīth collections, provide a wealth of material in which dreams are treated as authentic sources of knowledge; numerous individuals have dreams that foretell the future, and Muḥammad's Companions are portrayed as frequently asking him to interpret their dreams.

Between these bodies of literature, it seems noteworthy that the post-Qur'ānic sources give much greater attention to dreams and visions as routes for communication between metaphysical and physical worlds. The ḥadīth corpus tells us that to see Muḥammad in a dream means that one has really seen him, and that dreams provide the only trace of prophecy that can remain after Muḥammad's death—specifically, 1/46th of prophecy. These representations of dreams as a means for Muḥammad to remain present with his community, or for ordinary believers to share in a taste of prophetic experience after the final prophet has left this world, are nowhere to be found in the Qur'ān. Why would there be such disconnect between the sources?

While the Qur'ān's verses were revealed in real time through the body of a living prophet, addressing questions and controversies among his community as they arose, the ḥadīth traditions spoke to a post-prophetic community, a setting in which divine revelation had been silenced. Muslim traditions hold the Qur'ān to have been revealed entirely to Muḥammad in a twenty-three-year period. Secular scholarship lacks the evidence to support this faith conviction, but similarly lacks the evidence to deny it: at best, the field recognizes that the Qur'ān's organization into its recognizable form took place no later than the lifetime of Muḥammad's Companions. In contrast, our earliest textual sources on Muḥammad's biography and discourses appear two centuries after his death. Fred Donner has demonstrated meaningful departures in language and content between the sources, with which he argues that the Qur'ān and at least a significant portion of the ḥadīth corpus did not emerge in the same historical setting.[2] The Qur'ān's minimal offerings on the power of dreams, like its silence on political power struggles that divided Muslims after Muḥammad's death, might speak to the early codification of the Qur'ān—and conversely, the lateness of the ḥadīth traditions.

I am not an absolute skeptic regarding the authenticity question that haunts our ḥadīth sources; but even if we can reliably trace some narrations to Muḥammad's Companions, we must recognize that these Companions are speaking *after* Muḥammad's death, primarily to a younger generation that had not known him. Comparing the Qur'ān and ḥadīth sources, it appears that dreams served to ease the pain and crisis of a prophet-centered community that Muḥammad's death had rendered prophetless. Whether or not Muḥammad ever actually said that we could see him in dreams, it is easy to speculate as to why such an idea became immeasurably important, both for Muḥammad's Companions who longed for their departed prophet and for later generations who had never seen him with their own eyes.

The generations that followed the original Muslim community did not have the luxury of Muḥammad's likeness surviving in a photo archive. Among the networks of ḥadīth scholars that proliferated two centuries after the death of Muḥammad, therefore, we find a number of traditions in which Companions describe Muḥammad's physical appearance to those who had not witnessed him. These traditions offer details such as the length of Muḥammad's hair, the number of gray hairs in his beard, the dimensions of his torso, the nature of his stride, the shape of his face, and even the size of his joints. Several versions emphasize his body as perfectly proportioned and consistently moderate: neither too tall nor too short, his skin neither too light nor too dark, his hair neither too straight nor too curly. The conventional lens for interpreting these reports is that of devotion: people wanted to know what the Prophet looked like because he occupied such a central position in their hearts and religious imaginations. Of course, this isn't invalid: as paintings of Muḥammad were (mostly) absent from religious life, reproducing the textual descriptions of his appearance became modes of expressing love for him and transforming space with his simulated presence. But the precise accounts of Muḥammad's body can serve a different purpose when placed in conversation with Muḥammad's promise: "Whoever sees me in a dream has seen me, because the Devil cannot assume my form." The protection of Muḥammad from demonic impersonation added significance to his bodily details. If someone could really see and even communicate with the Prophet in a dream or vision, it would be important to correctly identify him; moreover, the possibility of directly witnessing Muḥammad was enhanced by imprinting his image on one's consciousness. Ṣūfī masters such as 'Abd al-Karīm Jīlī (d. 1403 CE) reproduced these textual descriptions of Muḥammad in their works and encouraged readers to imagine Muḥammad until attaining witness of him.[3]

If Muḥammad can guide us in dreams, the death of the final prophet does not mean the end of prophethood; throughout Muslim traditions, dreams appear as a means of divine guidance continuing even in the absence of a transcendent leader. In the tradition of Ithna 'Asharī Shī'ism, Muḥammad was succeeded as spiritual authority by a series of twelve righteous and divinely guided Imāms, consisting of his son-in-law, 'Alī ibn Abū Ṭālib, 'Alī's sons Ḥasan and Ḥusayn, and several generations of Ḥusayn's descendants. When the twelfth Imām disappeared from this world into a supernatural state of *ghaybat*, believers in this Imāmī lineage faced a crisis similar to that of the original Muslim community after the death of Muḥammad. However, parallel to the return of the Prophet in dreams, the missing twelfth Imām would appear to believers in their dreams and offer crucial guidance. As scholar Omid Ghaemmaghami points out, the Imām's physical description in these dreams as a *shābb* (youth) of overwhelming beauty and perfection overlaps with ḥadīth traditions that report Muḥammad witnessing God in the same form.[4] Theologians in both Sunnī and Shī'ī contexts wrestled with the possibility of seeing Allāh in dreams and visions, producing a multiplicity of opinions as well as personal testimonies; twelfth-century Ḥanbalī ḥadīth scholar Ibn al-Jawzī saw God in three separate dreams.[5]

If we want to imagine canonical texts as bastions of stability that properly anchor tradition and regulate doctrine, and visionary mysticism as offering only religious anarchy and the breakdown of coherence, the treatment of dreams in the Sunna presents a problem. The texts destabilize themselves; the canonical collections offer dreams as ways for Muḥammad to continue speaking to his community, which means that he can potentially undermine his own rules and meanings. But Muḥammad's appearances in dreams and visions, sought by traditionalists grounded in the texts, are not necessarily going to bring the whole edifice crumbling down; dream conversations with the Prophet can even draw someone closer to the texts and their laws. Of course, Muḥammad is not the only messenger in this realm. Dreamers can potentially communicate with a host of characters: other prophets, angels, Imāms, the mysterious figure of Khiḍr, scholars and saints of previous generations, essentially anyone who has left this world for the next, and potentially God himself, and all of these figures are capable of saying anything. They can tell you which legal school to follow, or whether you need to follow a school at all; they can uphold, suspend, or shatter laws, or take you to a place beyond questions of living inside or outside the law. The beauty and danger of dreams is that they can flow in any direction.

Dreamers and Scholars

It appears that dream interpretation enjoyed credibility as a science among the earliest Muslims, whether centered in Muḥammad's own acts of oneiocriticism or traditions of the surrounding milieu. Ibn al-Musayyib (d. 715), a ḥadīth scholar and jurist in Medina, was regarded as an expert on dreams, authorized by a teaching lineage with untouchable credentials: his mentor in the arts of dream interpretation, Asma' bint Abī Bakr, had been instructed by her father, Muḥammad's close Companion and the first caliph, Abū Bakr as-Siddīq.[6] Subsequent generations developed a science of Muslim dream interpretation, ta'bīr, amid the immense 'Abbāsid translation movement that brought Muslim rulers and intellectuals into conversation with Greek, Persian, and Indian literary heritages. The caliph al-Ma'mūn personally commissioned the rendering of the Greek *Oneirocritica* by Artemidorus of Ephesus into Arabic, and Muslim dream books frequently introduced their subject matter with adaptations of Greek dream theory.[7]

Though Sunnī intellectual tradition has been widely imagined as marked by obsession over textual authenticity, preserving the legacy of Muḥammad through rigorous critical evaluation of sayings and actions attributed to him, Sunnīsm's canon was also guided by dreams and visions. Beyond a master traditionist such as Bukhārī taking inspiration for his project from a dream of the

Prophet, ḥadīth scholars looked to their visionary experiences of Muḥammad or scholars of previous generations to determine the trustworthiness of ḥadīth transmitters. Seminal ḥadīth critic Aḥmad ibn Ḥanbal, for example, asked Muḥammad in a dream if everything that Abū Hurayra attributed to him was trustworthy. Though Abū Hurayra had spent limited time with Muḥammad, he produced an immense mountain of ḥadīth reports, including misogynistic claims that were denied and refuted by none other than Muḥammad's own widow 'Ā'isha. Muḥammad told Ibn Ḥanbal that everything from Abū Hurayra was reliable.[8]

Dreams could even turn scholars into saints, as dreams of deceased clerics could reveal their glorified status in the afterlife. Such dreams might undermine the division that we imagine between the textualism of "Wahhābī" scholarship and the visionary mystical knowledge of Ṣūfism. Aḥmad ibn Ḥanbal, eponym of the Ḥanbalī legal tradition, is commonly regarded today as an ideological grandfather of ugly modern fundamentalisms and thereby a staunch opponent of all things mystical. But in the generations after his death, Ibn Ḥanbal interacted with numerous individuals through their dreams. One dreamer witnessed Ibn Ḥanbal guarding the gates of paradise, the lone human guard among angels; others observed and reported Ibn Ḥanbal's powers of intercession. Still another saw Ibn Ḥanbal walking alongside Muḥammad; this vision served as a lesson to the dreamer, who was unable to catch up to them.[9] The appearances of Ibn Ḥanbal in dreams rendered him no longer merely a pious scholar who had lived and died in this world, but a supernatural being who could speak and bless from the realm of angels and prophets.

These dreams drew from and supported a logic regarding souls and their passage between worlds. For Ibn Qayyim al-

Jawzīyya, a prominent scholar in the Ḥanbalī tradition, dreams confirmed the existence of the soul and the afterlife. In accordance with the intellectual genealogies through which he became a master scholar, Ibn Qayyim taught that a ray of the soul emanated from the body during sleep. This soul-ray reaches into the heavens and returns to the body upon waking. During its travels, the sleeper's soul-ray can come into contact with other soul-rays and even the spirits of the dead, and through these encounters the person can obtain knowledge that s/he did not have access to in the waking world. The dreamer, Ibn Qayyim explains, can ask questions from the dead, and can even learn secrets about other living people that would have been unknowable otherwise. Ibn Qayyim himself benefited from this mode of knowledge, as the deceased Ibn Taymiyya appeared to him in a dream with the good news that Ibn Qayyim had nearly reached his own elite class of shaykhs.[10] However, during the soul-ray's flight, the dreamer also becomes vulnerable to the Devil (Shayṭān), who can mix this information with other materials to render the dream a source of confusion or anxiety. According to Ibn Qayyim, the soul-ray's emanation from the body during sleep—evidenced by reports of knowledge obtained by contact with the dead in dreams—proved that there was an aspect of the human being that could exist outside the body. In dreamers' communications with spirits of the dead, according to Ibn Qayyim, we have confirmation that human beings indeed have souls that occupy an alternate plane of existence after death.[11]

In her *Sufi Narratives of Intimacy: Ibn 'Arabī, Gender, and Sexuality*, scholar Sa'diyya Shaikh describes a dream of the Prophet experienced by revered Ḥanbalī jurist Ibn Taymiyya. For those who would pin modern problems of Islamist extremism, scriptural literalism, and the particular hyper-Sunnī project of the contemporary Saudi state on Ḥanbalism, Ibn Taymiyya popularly becomes a major figure in the chain, his works fueling the trends of modern revivalists. Not many people would read Ibn Taymiyya with the expectation of finding a feminist, but in a dream encounter, Ibn Taymiyya found his gender politics corrected by the Prophet. As the story goes, Ibn Taymiyya had grown so uncomfortable during the lecture of a woman scholar, Shaykha Fāṭima, that he did not hear a word that she had said. That night, however, he experienced a dream visit from Muḥammad, who told Ibn Taymiyya that Shaykha Fāṭima was a pious woman.[12] Throughout the history of normative, ḥadīth-centered, legalist Sunnī scholarly traditions, we find Muḥammad showing up to offer specific guidance from a place outside his textual traces.

Ibn Taymiyya's dream encounter produces a compelling tension. Ibn Taymiyya appears from his works as a staunch legalist and uncompromising opponent of religious innovation and deviation from established norms. As Alexander Knysh notes, "Ibn Taymiyya energetically denied any possibility for human beings to penetrate God's unfathomable mystery."[13] Ibn Taymiyya vehemently condemned mystics, philosophers, and sectarian movements that departed from what he regarded as the clearly drawn boundaries of authentic Islamic knowledge. Ibn Taymiyya's legacy in the modern world is complex and controversial: many see him as a much-needed reviver of the original and authentic Islam, the way of the Salaf; others consider his influence to represent everything that has gone wrong with Islam. He is far and away the most promoted classical thinker in Saudi Arabia, and his name frequently appears in genealogies of modern fundamentalisms, cited as a crucial influence on the likes of Osama bin Laden and ISIS.

In particular relevance for this chapter, Ibn Taymiyya's thought is often treated as the most historically significant opposition to Ṣūfism of lawless and/or pantheistic varieties, as well as the culture of local shrines and veneration for the tombs of holy people. Despite his ostensible skepticism and traditionalist hostility toward mystical knowledge, however, Ibn Taymiyya could not deny ways of knowing that betrayed both the rational and scriptural routes. The Prophet's visit to Ibn Taymiyya in his dream potentially blows a hole in the wall of Ibn Taymiyya's system—even if there is nothing about the hole itself that violates Ibn Taymiyya's personal constructions of orthodoxy. The sources that Ibn Taymiyya regards as supremely authentic, after all, taught him that Muḥammad could appear in dreams and communicate directly with dreamers.

Sa'diyya Shaikh observes, "No less than a vision of the Prophet himself allayed Ibn Taymiyya's prejudice and annoyance at a woman's assumption of public ritual leadership."[14] Ibn Taymiyya, a jurist desiring coherence and stability, does not appear to have crawled through the hole in his wall to explore whatever weird and threatening worlds existed beyond his system. But as a line of flight, this break in the wall remains unrepaired for those who wish to use it, even if only as a temporary relief from the structure. This break might lead to new resources as attempts to locate our own world's notions of justice and mercy in the world of a seventh-century revelation become increasingly frustrating. In her work *Inside the Gender Jihad*, Amina Wadud upholds the divine status of the Qur'ānic text while also calling for us to reconsider the various limits that we place on Allāh's ability to speak. In *Feminist Edges of the Qur'ān*, Aysha Hidayatullah considers the consequences of pursuing justice as defined "beyond" the text of the Qur'ān, asking hard questions: "What does it mean to stop handing ultimate authority to the text in this particular way . . . In what way is the text still divine?"[15] When academically trained exegesis and (post)modern theories of scriptural hermeneutics fail to rehabilitate the sacred sources, a feminist and queer-affirming Muslim feminism might come to us in our dreams. If those of us who want such openings exist outside the pale of tradition, as tradition's self-appointed protectors so often tell us, perhaps it is only from our dreams that the new books will come.

Dreams of Muḥammad and other holy figures both drew from the textual corpus and contributed to it. Practitioners who were blessed with dream encounters not only provided reports of their interactions with the dead, but sometimes produced entire books that they claimed to have *received* through these encounters, rather than *authored* with their own pens and ideas. In the most famous example, Andalusian mystical theologian Ibn al-'Arabī offered his *Fuṣūṣ al-Hikma* not as his personal project, but as a supernaturally revealed text that had been delivered to him in its entirety from Muḥammad in a dream. For Ibn Taymiyya, the interpretations furthered in Ibn al-'Arabī's *Fuṣūṣ* develop and promote the dangerous doctrine of "unificationism" (*ittiḥād*), which Ibn Taymiyya relates to incarnationism and unbelief.[16] According to Ibn Taymiyya and other opponents, the arcane, allegorical, and sometimes wildly counterintuitive readings of the Qur'ān and ḥadīth traditions found in the *Fuṣūṣ* position Ibn al-'Arabī as an outright denier of the plain content of the sacred sources. Readers who regard Ibn al-'Arabī's visionary experiences as legitimate, however, recognize his *Fuṣūṣ* as a sacred source in its own right. Sa'diyya Shaikh writes about Ibn al-'Arabī's mystical theology as a potential resource for rethinking gender in Islam, while recognizing that the shaykh remains a product of his specific time and place.

Perhaps we can benefit from an exploration not only of Ibn al-'Arabī's readings, but also the methods by which he achieved and authorized his readings. Perhaps a new *Fuṣūṣ* is waiting to be revealed.

Ibn al-'Arabī's followers and admirers call him Shaykh al-Akbar, the "Greatest Shaykh," his detractors label him Shaykh al-Akfar, the "Most Unbelieving Shaykh." While Ibn al-'Arabī might not provide the most fruitful endorsement for dreams as literary sources, depending on who you ask, scholars with more street cred in neotraditionalist circles also produced new works from their dream encounters. Shāh Walī Allāh Dihlawī, the eighteenth-century Indian scholar who is regarded as a crucial reviver and defender of Islam for his era, gets floated around today as an exemplar of the Muslim intellectual who balances rationalist critiques with mastery of ḥadīth scholarship. What gets excluded from this image of Shāh Walī Allāh is the shaykh's investment in dreams and visions. Shāh Walī Allāh's valorization of transmitted knowledge drew from the authority of suprarational dream knowledge: on behalf of Bukhārī, Shāh Walī Allāh tells us of a pious man's dream in which Muḥammad told him to step back from preoccupation with Shāfi'ī jurisprudence and turn toward Bukhārī's collection.[17] Shah Walī Allāh also reports of his own mystical life, which includes visions of Muḥammad, who would personally answer his questions. He was visited in dreams by Muḥammad's grandsons Ḥasan and Ḥusayn, who repaired a broken pen for him and clothed him in the robe of their grandfather.[18] These interactions informed Shah Walī Allāh's personal trajectory, providing him with compelling religious content in the form of individualized guidance from the Prophet.

Shah Walī Allāh referred to scholarly consensus to affirm that using dream interpretation to tell the future, as in the cases of astrology, geomancy, and other technologies, was forbidden by divine law.[19] But dreams were still real and played a vital role in his system. While emphasizing the importance of the Prophet as a perfect guide for deficient seekers, Shah Walī Allāh empowers seekers to consider forms of revelation as ongoing and within their reach, if only they pay attention: "There is no human individual who lacks the capacity to attain the unseen through a dream which he has, a vision that he sees, a voice from the unseen which he hears, or an intuition which he recognizes."[20]

Mystics, Anti-Mystics, and Mystical Anti-Mystics

Dreams and visions grounded in devotion to Allāh, Muḥammad, his family, and the sages of the past, as well as deep Muslim traditions of dream interpretation and visionary practices, can be conceptualized as no less "Islamic" than any ritual act or method of interpretation. To hold a stake in the power of dreams—even the power of Muḥammad to visit believers in their dreams—is endorsed by the most canonical sources and the lives of seminal Muslim scholars. Dreams are so deeply entrenched in Muslim traditions that we can find them on both sides of any sectarian or philosophical debate; dreaming offers a point of intersection and shared resource between neotraditionalists and mystics, "Wahhābī" and "Ṣūfī" Muslims.

Modern reformers such as the nineteenth/twentieth-century proto-Salafī intellectual Rashīd Riḍā turned away from dreams as routes of communication with the unseen; Riḍā generally disdained dreams as part of his attack on Ṣūfīs as irrational and superstitious enemies of Muslims' civilizational progress, either playing tricks on the masses or having themselves fallen under deception by devils.[21] In modern Saudi Arabia, however, despite the ongoing science-ish vision of Sunnī Islam as a pure body of empirically authenticated textual knowledge handed down in scholarly lineages, religious projects can still be driven by dreams. Muhsin Khan, whose translations of the Qur'ān and ḥadīth collections are presently favored by the Saudi government's media complexes, was not a trained religious scholar or linguist, but a medical doctor who came to Medina to work at the Islamic University's hospital in the 1960s. Khan was not a particularly pious person at the time, but found himself transformed by a dream in which he visualized Muḥammad. In the dream, Khan witnessed Muḥammad sweating profusely, and decided to help the Prophet by drinking the sweat. Disturbed and confused by the dream, Khan was fortunate to be living in the city of the Prophet, where he could seek out the seminal traditionalist scholars of his age. Khan asked Ibn Baz, one of the greatest Salafī or "Wahhābī" scholars of the twentieth century as well as a noted dream interpreter, for help in understanding the image. Ibn Baz told Khan that the dream signified his calling to do service to the Prophet and Islam. Khan's dream of drinking prophetic sweat, and its analysis by one of the world's premier neotraditionalist dream interpreters, pushed Khan toward a project of translating the Qur'ān and Bukhārī's ḥadīth collection. Khan's Qur'ān translation, now printed in the millions and distributed worldwide by the Saudi government, is famously intolerant toward not only other religious confessions but even Muslims who do not conform to Saudi Arabia's state version of Sunnism. Many Muslims find his translation particularly embarrassing for the ways in which Khan inserts his own commentary into the English verses, essentially disguising his personal interpretations as part of the original Qur'ān. What's interesting about Khan's experience is that some might assume the official "Wahhābism" of the Saudi state to be staunchly anti-mystical; at the very least, critics of Muhsin Khan's Qur'ān translation aren't likely to imagine him as a mystical thinker.

While fully "orthodox" in theory, dreams and visions can also offer tunnels out of the power relations and textualist structures that make such a thing as "orthodoxy" conceptually possible. Dreams are anti-structure, operating within their own logic or against logic, undoing coherence. These visionary experiences unsettle and destabilize; they present the message of Islam not as a fixed and concretized artifact of textual transmission, but as eternally malleable, a conversation with Muḥammad that has not ended. Moreover, dreams allow for multiple conversations: taking our dreams seriously means not only that Muḥammad continues to speak, but that he can say different things to different people. Dreams restore us to the fluidity of the original Muslim community, in which massive books of jurisprudence were unnecessary because Muslims enjoyed the presence of a living prophet and divine revelation that could descend at any time.

Naturally, clerical scholars would argue for limits on what dreams and visions can actually do, and reject dreams as the basis for new legal norms. Ṣūfī master 'Abd al-Qādir al-Jilānī narrates that when he dreamed of a light telling him that forbidden acts had been made permissible for him, he immediately recognized the light as the Devil, who sought to deceive him.[22] Religious scholars would commonly warn that dream interpretation by the untrained threatens to lead the dreamer astray; for better or worse, dreams can lead a dreamer out of the scholars' hands. Muḥammad himself can appear in a dream and tell the dreamer to trust herself even against the consensus of the 'ulama. Though dream visits from Muḥammad might leave the public law unchanged, they can enable a more complex relationship between the word of the law and the heart of the Prophet: dreams can affirm with Muḥammad's own voice that not every "illegal" act necessarily constitutes a "sin." This possibility can offer something when the problem of law isn't actually its status as *law*, but a problem of theology and ontology. For many of us hurt by the famous "wife-beating" verse, 4:34, the crisis is not only or even primarily a legal one; we are not all in the trenches or dealing with 4:34 as a physical effect in the world, whether in courts or communities. Rather, many readers of 4:34 struggle with what they could consider its spiritual consequences: we are heartbroken by the Qur'ān's presentation of Allāh as a patriarchal misogynist who gives divine approval to domestic violence. This ontological challenge of 4:34 cannot be helped by a close examination of premodern Ottoman court cases, because even the most compassionate human jurists can only go so far toward undoing the words; frankly, we want Allāh to say something else. If the verse is not going to change, perhaps the author can give some new clarification.

Dreams can bring healing to those who find themselves hurt by the law. A poignant example comes from the life of Muḥammad, following the mass exodus of Muslims from the hostile environment of Mecca to the city of Medina. The ḥadīth corpus reports of one Muslim refugee, unable to withstand the extreme loneliness, homesickness, and unfamiliar climate that he experienced in Medina, making the decision to take his own life. Numerous ḥadīths report Muḥammad's condemnation and promises of otherworldly punishments for one who commits suicide, but the man's friend nonetheless saw him in a dream, wearing bandages over his wounds but apparently in paradise. The deceased told his friend that Allāh had forgiven him and brought him into the garden. Upon waking, the friend reported his dream to Muḥammad, who endorsed the vision as valid. For a friend devastated by grief, the dream provided a solace that even numerous prophetic statements about Allāh's boundless mercy and compassion could not have offered. Through its allowance of dreams as communication between metaphysical and physical realms, the textual corpus still provides routes to that solace.

A dream of Muḥammad comforted me at a time when I believed that I was leaving Islam forever. Sharing an embrace in my dream with the Prophet, 'Alī, and the leaders of the youths of paradise, Ḥasan and Ḥusayn, took place at the perfect moment (right after I had mistreated a Qur'ān, in fact) and became a new text for me to consider. The love and acceptance that I felt in our encounter kept me open to a future relationship with the Qur'ān; the dream restored the Qur'ān in ways that the Qur'ān, at least to my eyes at that time, could not have achieved for itself. Nor could the imāms and scholars whom I trusted as authoritative experts and pious exemplars have given me the sublime consolation of what I experienced as Muḥammad's own hands. My dream of Muḥammad's embrace could be related to the classical model of dreams as devices of authorization, though it only served to authorize me to my own self. From one point of view, I was living outside the tradition; but through the dream, resources within the tradition still validated my right to self-care. The appearance of Muḥammad and his family transformed my attempted apostasy into a deeply Islamic act.

In modern contexts, despite the traditionalist credibility of dreams, many Muslims would take discomfort with the notion of dreams as meaningful sources of religious guidance. Even if the great scholar Bukhārī and his ilk relied on dreams, modern believers might imagine a clear opposition between the entirely personal, subjective, and irrational content of dreams and the textualist emphasis on authentic sources. To denounce dreams and visions in favor of textual transmissions, however, might provoke a difficult conversation about where and when we decide to valorize rationality as a religious value. Islam, after all, does not begin with Muḥammad as a university-educated scholar, formulating reasoned arguments based on his rigorous study of texts; rather, Muḥammad was a mystic visionary and famously unlettered, and his prophetic vocation began with dreams. The only portion of prophethood that would survive after him, he is reported to have said, consisted of true dreams. While Muḥammad is also supposed to have called scholars the "heirs of prophets," dreamers and ecstatic visionaries are the ones who share in his method.

All of the later scholarly machinations that sought to scrutinize narrations about Muḥammad for historical accuracy, guard the Qur'ān's clear content against sectarians and charismatic charlatans who sought to distort the revelation, and present Islam as a coherent textualist system with clear and reliably drawn boundaries continue to rest on the Prophet's foundation of visions, voices, and dreams. Many of us would rather not think about this; some prefer to relegate the visionary aspect of Islam to its origins and experience Islam instead as a collection of words on paper, a mountain of doctrinal positions and legal rulings. Despite the prominence of dreams in the history of Sunnī traditionalism (and even contemporary figures such as Muhsin Khan), some Saudi scholars would offer dismissals of dream interpretation as Ṣūfī "superstition" in contrast to the supposed textual integrity of their own lineage. This way of thinking about Islam, however, is not the only game in town, nor can it claim to represent Islam's inevitable and organic center. When we leave ourselves open to visionary encounters, there is no center—or the center is *us*.

I am not especially interested or invested in the question of whether dreams come to us from some transcendent power "out there" or from within our own brains. Dreams and chemically assisted visions have contributed to my experience of living as a Muslim, informing the ways that I think about the sacred sources and the multiple Muslim communities with whom I share in them. The tradition gives me tools for reading my dreams, while simultaneously authorizing my dreams as escape routes from its own walls when needed. Through dreams and drugs, the tradition becomes fluid, capable of movement and mutation, fragmentation and departure, but also return; and even when visionary experiences provide a way out, they also bring me back in. The Prophet's daughter told me to leave the Qur'ān alone and listen to her instead, but the relief and peace that she provided ultimately restored my capacity for sitting with the Qur'ān. Sometimes, dreaming's power of deconstruction can even help to hold it all together.

7

Coming of the Black God: Esoteric Revival and American Islam

> We have the roots of everything. We have the root of the universe. I don't want you to get excited and throw stones at me, because I speak of that which you never dreamed of hearing; however, it is the truth.
>
> —ELIJAH MUHAMMAD[1]

In *Black Magic*, Yvonne P. Chireau presents a conventional binary of magic and religion—magical spells are mechanical and personal, while religious prayer is devotional and communal—that quickly collapses under critical scrutiny.[2] While holding on to this binary, however, Chireau admits that it's not helpful when looking at histories of African American religion and traditions of Conjure, Hoodoo, and root work, whose practitioners were often Christian ministers or church members and who understood these technologies through a biblical lens.[3] Chireau reaches the conclusion that in Black folk traditions, "religion" and "magic" are not always distinct, but often complementary categories.[4]

A closer look at Black folk traditions confuses not only our boundaries between religion and magic, but also imaginary separations between "African American religion" and other histories. European Christians, for example, brought their own concepts of supernatural forces (and ways of working with these forces) to the Americas, and these concepts entered into exchange with African religion. Chireau argues that Anglo-American ideas and practices were often compatible with West African traditions, and that enslaved Africans adopted European magic along with evangelical Christianity, bringing both into conversation with their own knowledge and practice.[5] Anglo investments in the supernatural were evidenced not only by events such as the white hysteria of the Salem witchcraft trials but also by the apparent terror with which white plantation owners regarded African sorcery. Black conjurers were known to use their skills to assist slave rebellions; the famed Gullah Jack, for example, provided rebels in Denmark Vesey's planned revolt with crab claw charms that he believed would make them impervious to white violence. Slaves sometimes used the threat of sorcery as a means of resistance against the cruelty of slave owners, who took these threats seriously; anxious whites even passed laws to prohibit Africans from practicing their herb technologies. In plantation cultures, the sharing of stories between children of slaves and children of slave owners could also have helped to produce a mutual understanding of the supernatural world.[6]

At the collision of European and African traditions in American slavery, we can witness the racialization of magic as a concept. In white Christian imaginaries, the indigenous practices of Black people could not rightfully be called "religion," but belonged to a primitive and more sinister category. For white Christians, *every* African means of engaging supernatural powers amounted to idolatry and witchcraft. Living under white power, some enslaved Africans and their descendants appeared to have internalized these narratives, leading to an increasing anxiety over the threat of "antisocial magic" in African American religious traditions.[7]

Further confusing both the religion-magic binary and assumed separations between religions, we have reason to believe that Muslim practices contributed to what could be called African magic in the Americas. In West Africa, Muslim holy men provided goods and services, such as protective Qur'ānic talismans and healing prayers, to both Muslims and non-Muslims. In his history of American Muslims, Kambiz GhaneaBassiri speculates that these practices could have continued among enslaved African Muslims in the Americas.[8] For GhaneaBassiri, the powers of Muslim holy men and artifacts such as Qur'ān amulets reveal the polysemous nature of religious life in African communities on both sides of the Atlantic.[9]

Throughout the later nineteenth century, the surge of interest in esotericism, occultism, and metaphysical religion in Victorian America occasionally led to encounters with Islam. In 1873, a spiritualist medium claimed to have received a visit from the Prophet Muḥammad, who disavowed his past "pagan worship" and fully endorsed the spiritualist movement[10]; in the 1890s, a white Theosophist named Alexander Russell Webb converted to Islam without ever giving up Theosophy, arguing that Islam offered a perfect expression of Theosophical ideals.[11] The Shriners claimed Bektashi affiliation and a chain of transmitted authority that began with

'Alī, son-in-law of the Prophet. In the first decades of the twentieth century, the earliest transnational Muslim missionaries to America, representatives of the Ahmadiyya movement that had originated in colonial India, interacted with Freemasons and metaphysical groups. Hazrat Inayat Khan, pioneering ambassador of Ṣūfism to the West, carefully branded his particular Ṣūfism to match trends in alternative American spirituality, alongside groups that offered similar reconstructions of Hinduism.

In the cities of the northeastern United States during the years between the World Wars, Islam would again become an ingredient in African American matrices of sacred powers. In this setting, Islam attained its values and meanings through collisions and cross-fertilizations with numerous resources and traditions, including Freemasonry, Theosophy, broader nineteenth-century occult revivals, popular magic literatures and products, various Christian and Black Israelite movements that sought to reclaim lost histories and sacred futures for Black people, and growing American fascination with all things "Oriental." There were also Muslim leaders and movements, as well as non-Muslims who praised Islam for its reported racial egalitarianism, but this eclecticism and admixture leads many Muslims and non-Muslims alike to question whether the end product can be rightfully called "Islamic" at all. Throughout the explorations of what some would call African American "proto-Islamic" movements, it should be clear that I have no interest in attempting to patrol the limits of Islamic authenticity or "orthodoxy"; if anything, I want to dig secret tunnels or find holes in the fences. There are many ways to trace the history of American Islam, particularly the African American Muslim traditions examined here, and a variety of choices for how we map this history in relation to broader American religion.

In discussions of American religious history, as Catherine Albanese has noted, esotericism and occultism typically become the socks that get lost in the laundry.[12] The history of American religion, however, is more than the history of mainline white Protestant churches. Likewise, the history of American Islam is more than the transplanting of "classical Sunnī tradition" into a new setting or the supposed "disguising" of secular Black nationalism in religiously Islamic costume. Esotericism and the occult are left out of American religious histories, Muslims are also neglected as genuine participants in American religion, and discussions of Muslims tend to produce an artificial monolith all its own. These exclusions and marginalizations lead to the intersection of esotericism and Islam in the United States being triply ignored, though this intersection is precisely what gives us American Islam in its recognizable history.

From Magical Art to Moorish Science

Advertisements in African American newspapers of the early twentieth century witnessed a thriving industry of books and products that promised access to unseen powers: spell books, charms, rings, herbs, "luck bags," and "magnetic loadstones." These items were often marketed as originating from a mystical, magical East. A major figure in the new magic industry, William de Laurence, was a white man from Ohio who presented himself as a world traveler, collector of rare texts and artifacts, and expert scholar of occult practices found throughout the "Orient." At the start of the twentieth century, he established the De Laurence Institute of Hypnotism and Occult Philosophy in Chicago and published *The Book of Magical Art*, later expanded and retitled *The Book of Magical Art, Hindu Ritual and Indian Occultism.* Selling books, powders, oils, and other occult artifacts via his De Laurence Company catalogs and advertisements in Black newspapers, de Laurence developed a reputation as the "world's finest magician" and a "superguru."[13] He found particular success among Jamaican readers:[14] his works were read avidly by Rastafarians in the 1930s, and his own invented formulas managed to supplant indigenous versions.[15] On the other side of the Black Atlantic, a Nigerian teenager was so inspired by de Laurence's products and literature that he journeyed to the United States to study under him.

The popularity of de Laurence's catalogs speaks to the tensions that Randall Styers has observed in the construction of "magic" as a category in the late nineteenth and early twentieth centuries, particularly its relationship to "science," anxieties over marking the boundaries of the "modern," and the significance of these terms in European colonialism.[16] Mitch Horowitz, examining the wild success of this turban-wearing blond man from Ohio in marketing magic to Afro-Caribbean audiences, suggests that de Laurence's location in "the heartland of America, a nation that still had the majestic sheen of promise and progress," might have contributed to his appeal.[17] As his formal "institute" also boasted the gravitas of verifiable science, de Laurence's success confused the easy divisions of rationality vs. superstition, or modern vs. antimodern; his magic was completely modern, playing by modern rules, and authorizing itself through modern structures. When selling "Indian Occultism" to Black consumers, de Laurence also marketed magic within the logic of colonialism: he promoted the "Orient" as a resource of ancient magic and wonder, but also privileged himself as qualified to work as its proper custodian and expert. Appearing in his books as a white man wearing robes and other "Eastern" garb, sometimes with a star and crescent on his turban, he simultaneously expressed both magical Eastern wisdom and his rational Western mastery over it.

De Laurence entered into multiple intellectual genealogies with his publication in English of the mysterious grimoire *The 6th and 7th Books of Moses*. Through de Laurence's marketing efforts, the text became widely circulated throughout the Afro-Atlantic, and also reached major figures such as Rabbi Wentworth Matthew, early Black Israelite leader, and Leonard Howell, regarded as the founder of Rastafarian tradition.[18] Henri Gamache's 1945 sequel, *The 8th, 9th, and 10th Books of Moses*, centers his preface on the African contribution to Jewish religion, and presents Moses as "The Great Voodoo man of the Bible," demonstrating the cultural significance that the original text had accumulated over time.[19]

The author and origins of *The 6th and 7th Books of Moses* are unknown, but it has been suggested that the text first saw print in Germany in 1797.[20] Attribution of the text to Moses speaks to his long-standing depiction as master conjurer who outperforms sorcerers at their own game. In its provocative title, the text presents itself as a recovery of lost portions of Moses's contribution to the canonical Torah, a claim that resonates strongly with the antebellum traditions of "invisible churches." When slaves' scriptural knowledge was regulated by their masters, underground discourses claimed that the white man's Bible could not have been the entire scripture—that it had been corrupted or purged of elements that could become tools of liberation. In Jamaica, the colonial regime gave this potential meaning for *The 6th and 7th Books of Moses* even greater potency by officially banning the book, rendering its possession a criminal offense. Turning this collection of incantations and diagrams of amulets into contraband, the government unintentionally legitimized reading *The 6th and 7th Books of Moses* as an act of resistance against white power.

Another de Laurence publication, the "ancient Piece of Eastern Instruction" *Infinite Wisdom* (1923), was simultaneously published as *Unto Thee I Grant* by the Ancient and Mystical Order of the Rosae Crucis (AMORC), the American Rosicrucians. The text presents itself as having been authored circa 1350 BCE by the pharaoh Amenhotep IV, aka Akhenaton (himself a mystery-school initiate, philosopher, and famously monotheist), and recovered by the Rosicrucians' ahistorical founder, Christian Rosenkreuz. The earliest form of the text, however, appears to have been published in eighteenth-century England as *The Economy of Human Life*; this work, while appearing "distinctly bourgeois and Anglican in tone and content," was claimed to have been translated from an "Indian manuscript written by an ancient Brahmin."[21] In the 1920s, the text would in turn undergo appropriation as a key ingredient in a new American Muslim scripture, *The Holy Koran of the Moorish Science Temple of America*, known popularly as the *Circle Seven Koran*.

By what historical processes could a European text, reconstituted as a Masonic manuscript, attributed to an ancient Egyptian pharaoh, and distributed by white men become positioned as an Islamic source for Black freedom struggle? And how would one measure the "Islam" that comes through these processes? How do we understand this *Circle Seven Koran*?

The *Circle Seven Koran* emerged as a dynamic point of intersection between various flows of materials. The emerging body of popular grimoires and mail-order occult Orientalism of figures such as de Laurence shared space with numerous practitioners who advertised their services in Black newspapers. Like the books and products, these practitioners typically claimed authorization from the traditions of an exotic East, either as travelers who had returned to America with secret knowledges or as natives introducing their previously unknown homeland traditions to the West. These practitioners often merged occult "Hindoo" traditions, secrets of pharaonic Egypt, and healing practices of Western Africa together into one vast, undifferentiated realm of magic and mystery. Legitimizing their Eastern knowledges with Western markers of authority, they claimed titles of "Doctor" and "Professor."

These practitioners sometimes claimed titles such as "Mohammedan Scientist" and origins in Muslim-majority societies.[22] Their advertisements also presented Islam as linked to Africanity, as in Professor Mormordoo's 1924 ad for an "African Lucky Ring, a rare product of African mysticism worn by privileged African Mohammedans only . . . For the first time in the history of African Occultism, this ring has been permitted to leave its African home and cross the waters."[23] One Mohammedan Scientist, going by a succession of names and titles throughout the 1920s, claimed mastery of "African and Oriental Occultism, Psychic Science, White and Black Magic, etc.," and appeared in papers such as the *Amsterdam News* and *Chicago Defender* wearing turbans and fezzes. Variously known as "Professor Akpan Aga, Wonderful Magician by Alchemy and Fire," Professor Akpandac, Professor Edeteffiong, Edet Effiong, "Effiong Offiong, of the Nigerian Remedy Company, Dealer in Roots and Herbs," or a "Mohammedan Master of Stricter African Science," he also switched points of religious emphasis, in some ads appearing more Christian or

Muslim than in others. Jacob S. Dorman suggests that he was probably also Professor Akpan Essien, the "mystery healer of the Mohammedan cult" who was arrested for unlicensed practicing of medicine and whose given name was revealed to be Thomas Williams.[24] In 1918, roughly contemporary to Akpandac, newspaper ads in Newark promoted "Professor Drew, the Egyptian Adept" and his healing powers. (He would share the title with another "Egyptian Adept," Hamid Bey of the Bey magicians' troupe, a team of Egyptian Copts who performed in 1920s New Jersey.[25]) The ads describe Professor Drew as a man "born with Divine power" who had been taught by the "Adepts of Egypt," and express his emphatic declaration, "I am a Moslem."[26]

If the American Dream is defined by the ability to reinvent yourself on your own terms and transcend your origins, Akpandac and Drew could be understood as Black inversions of *The Great Gatsby*. As Jay Gatz changed his name to *de*particularize, shedding any trace of ethnic difference for rebirth as Gatsby within a generic, universal whiteness, Akpandac and Drew sought to transcend their Blackness for identities that were *more* foreign and signified greater difference from the limited parameters of the white world. For many of these practitioners, claiming origins and knowledges in the East served as an escape route out of marginalized and discredited American Blackness into new identities that, while not fully privileged as "white," at least positioned them beyond the constraints of "Negro." An example would be the South Asian peddlers in early twentieth-century American cities who would play upon white customers' Orientalist fantasies to sell their goods, and African American peddlers who performed South Asian accents and fabricated exotic backstories to achieve the same access.[27] In a white supremacist society, "Oriental magic" became a mode of cultural and economic mobility.

In the second half of the 1920s, Professor Drew the Egyptian Adept resurfaced in Chicago with a new identity: Noble Drew Ali, Prophet of the Moorish Science Temple of America. Appearing in turbans, fezzes, and sashes reminiscent of Masonic regalia (the title of "Noble" itself recalled Freemasonry) and placing his hand on his chest to form a 7 with his body, he claimed to have received initiation at the Egyptian pyramids and that he was the appointed prophet who would restore African Americans to their true Moorish identity and creed. Like the other Egyptian Adept, Hamid Bey, Noble Drew Ali performed marvelous feats such as rope escape. Alongside practitioners selling their goods, lucky numbers, and occult services in Black newspapers of the period, his Moorish Manufacturing Corporation marketed a variety of "Moorish herb products" as cures for a variety of ailments: Moorish Antiseptic Bath Compound; Moorish Body Builder and Blood Purifier; Moorish Mineral and Healing Oil.[28] Like "Mohammedan Scientist" Akpandac/Effiong/Essien (Thomas Williams), Noble Drew Ali claimed knowledge of Jesus Christ's lost years in India.

Narratives asserting that Jesus had studied under Indian masters at some point in the eighteen "lost" years of his life that are not discussed in the canonical Gospels had grown popular since the second half of the nineteenth century. Russian writer Nicolas Notovitch claimed that while traveling in northern Indian Kashmir along the Tibetan border, he heard references to a grand lama known as Issa and ultimately discovered a biography of this lama at the monastery of Hemis. In 1890, Notovitch produced his translation of the text as *The Unknown Life of Jesus Christ*, portraying Jesus Christ's travels in the Punjab and Himalayas and his studies of Vedic literatures and Buddhism. The Jesus of this text condemns priesthoods, animal sacrifices, "heathen" idol worship, and miracles, at times reading as potentially Buddhist but overwhelmingly expressing the kind of rationalizing monotheism that a nineteenth-century European Protestant would construct.[29] Despite its dubious historicity, the text popularized interest in Jesus's lost years and the potential for him to have studied in mystery schools. In 1908, Levi H. Dowling published his *Aquarian Gospel of Jesus the Christ*, which he claimed to have produced through revelatory access to the Akashic records. In addition to placing the Jesus-in-India mythic history in conversation with early New Age notions of the coming "Age of Aquarius," Dowling's portrayal of Jesus consuming knowledge at the feet of masters in not only India but Persia, Greece, Assyria, Tibet, and Egypt serves to reframe Jesus's attainment of Christhood in New Thought terms. In Dowling's representation, Jesus *becomes* Christ through a process of self-perfection, rigorous study, and initiation. This is the Christ of Akpandac's thought: "When the statement is made that Christ was a Master, it means, literally speaking, that Christ was Master of Himself, educated and trod the path, receiving the instruction of the Masters in India and the Orient."[30]

For esotericist circles, the Jesus-in-India narrative produced a number of benefits: it allowed a variety of materials to find legitimation on Christian terms; it affirmed that Jesus's teachings contained esoteric elements that were either too advanced for common believers or actively suppressed by church authorities who found them threatening; it rationalized perceived parallels between Christianity and Buddhism; and it promoted the concept of a universal *philosophia perennis* that lay at the heart of all religions.[31] For Noble Drew Ali and the Mohammedan Scientist, Jesus in India could do all of that and more: the narrative allows for Jesus and his *true* teachings—which have been denied, erased, and misrepresented by the same European churches that happened to be complicit in the theft of African heritages, identities, and bodies—to be relocated in the Black and brown worlds. For a southern migrant such as Noble Drew Ali, perhaps versed in the oral traditions dating back to invisible churches, the claim that white men had suppressed the true teachings of Christ was nothing new. In this context, Jesus's tutelage in India offered consequences that white esotericists would not have foreseen.

These new constructions of Jesus as a student under Indian masters could also cross-pollinate with older imaginaries in Black Freemasonry that represented Moses as an initiate of Egyptian mystery schools, which served to locate both Freemasonry and biblical tradition as products of Africa. "Had Moses or the Israelites never lived in Africa," argues Martin Robison Delany in 1853, "the mysteries of the wise men of the East never would have been handed down to us."[32] Alexander Crummell (1819–98) likewise writes of ancient Egyptians as having been civilizing influences upon Moses and the Hebrews.[33]

Without attribution, Noble Drew Ali's *Circle Seven Koran* consists of wholesale cutting-and-pasting from Dowling's *Aquarian Gospel* and *Unto Thee I Grant*, causing a scholar to describe Noble Drew Ali as potentially "one of the more significant plagiarists of the twentieth century."[34] Apart from ideologically salient edits (replacing "God" with "Allah" and removing a description of young Jesus as "fair-haired boy, with deep blue eyes"), the *Circle Seven Koran* reproduces its sources. Moorish Science, building from this textual foundation, preserves major themes of New Thought: the immanence of God in the human soul, vision of heaven and hell as related to this world rather than an afterlife, esoteric universalism (as seen in Noble Drew Ali's inclusion of figures such as Buddha and Confucius within his roster of prophets), and a deep sense that established Christian churches have gotten Jesus very, very wrong, which had not only undermined humanity's spiritual progress but also resulted in mass enslavement and oppression.

What was the "science" in Noble Drew Ali's Moorish Science or the Mohammedan Science that Akpandac promoted? In the context of American esotericism, "science" meant a lot of things. Speaking to a world marked by perceived conflict between science and religion, esotericists often promised the means by which the two bodies of knowledge could be reconciled in harmony.[35] Moreover, "science" itself was malleable; "In the West Indies," writes Horowitz, "the term *science* sometimes connoted magical practices," as evidenced in references to science by Marcus Garvey.[36] As seen earlier in this discussion, practitioners would often advertise their services in American newspapers as "science," though this science consisted of methods that would now be termed magical or occult. Finally, there was also the proliferation of "science" as a buzzword in proto–New Thought through the contributions of Mary Baker Eddy, founder of Christian Science and regarded as an unintentional founding mother of New Thought at large.[37]

There are, of course, multiple genealogies that could be drawn for Moorish Science, depending on the relationships and connections that our specific eyes, driven by our values and prejudices, enable us to witness. Readers who focus on Noble Drew Ali's Islamic content might emphasize possible linkages to the Ahmadiyya movement or Dusé Mohamed Ali, or even consider a sustained Muslim consciousness among Africans in the Americas from the transatlantic slave trade all the way to the 1920s. Readers with an interest in Freemasonry can easily spot the aesthetics and performativity of the Shriners in Moorish Science regalia and pageantry, not to mention the direct presence of Rosicrucian texts. Those who want to see Moorish Science as both a cause and effect of Black freedom struggle might relate it primarily to similar movements among African Americans in cities of the post-migration North, such as Black Israelites, Garveyites, and a host of pan-Africanist groups. And those who wish to locate Noble Drew Ali as part of a broader esoteric tradition can do that as well: numerous white followers of Noble Drew Ali present him as chiefly a universalist or perennialist gnostic sage while unfortunately ignoring his legacy of Black resistance against white supremacy. When it comes to Moorish Science, people are going to see what they want to see, and any attempt at a family tree of lineal descent is going to leave out other possibilities.

Of course, the various lineages mentioned here are not isolated from each other. The Ahmadiyya movement, originating in late nineteenth-century India under British colonialism, developed alongside the "Jesus in India" narrative as it emerged in English sources. In the United States in the 1920s, Ahmadiyya missionaries became deeply entrenched in New Thought scenes, with leading Ahmadi personalities boasting degrees in metaphysical sciences from New Thought institutes. The Ahmadiyya also had a presence in Marcus Garvey's Universal Negro Improvement Association. Garvey, in turn, drew from New Thought and treated its principles as invaluable to racial uplift.[38] Garvey also took inspiration from the theatricality of Shriners; while the intersection of Freemasonry and esotericism needs no further elaboration here, it should also be repeated that the Shriners claimed a lineage from Bektashi Ṣūfīs. With Moorish Science, we're not getting a clean lineage of A→B→C but a complicated tangle of connections, with each of the connections forming connections to each other. There is no singular "original context" that sufficiently explains Moorish Science, whether that context be Black nationalism, New Age, or transnational Islam.

Magnets, Mathematics, and Arm-Leg-Leg-Arm-Head

For those who wish to envision traditions as clear parents and children to each other, Noble Drew Ali's Moorish Science Temple serves as the required precursor to Elijah Muhammad's Nation of Islam. Just as some find it necessary to claim that Noble Drew Ali had been a former member of the Ahmadiyya, some need to imagine that Elijah Muhammad and/or his teacher, Master Fard Muhammad, must have been members of the Moorish Science Temple before establishing their own movement. Without definitive evidence for any of these speculations, we can at least say that the Nation of Islam, originating in 1930s Detroit and Chicago, was swimming in more or less the same pool of diverse materials as 1920s Moorish Science.

The Nation's own narrative of its origins goes as follows: Allāh came in the person of Master Fard Muhammad, who had been born in the holy city of Mecca in 1877, and appeared on the streets of Detroit in 1930. He taught that God was not a spirit or ghost, but rather the "Black Man of Asia," and that the Devil had deceived Black people into denying their own divinity and nature as righteous Muslims. After three and a half years of preaching and teaching, during which he suffered relentless persecution at the hands of local authorities, he decided that his work was complete. He left his fledgling community in the hands of his most trusted minister, whom he had named Elijah Muhammad.

Whatever his actual origins and identity might have been, Master Fard Muhammad had come and gone like a stranger. Theories abound regarding his background and archive of sources; evidence suggests that he claimed to have come from Afghanistan on his draft registration card, but we know nothing of the books that he read. For the purposes of this project, one of the more tantalizing but unconfirmed speculations suggests that prior to his work in Detroit, he had been involved with both Marcus Garvey's UNIA and the Theosophical Society.[39] It is particularly difficult to distinguish between what Fard Muhammad himself had taught and what of NOI doctrine reflects the elaborations of his student, Elijah Muhammad. It does appear that the notion of Fard Muhammad as Allāh in person did not originate with Fard, who apparently had claimed mere prophethood as his station. Burnsteen Sharrieff Muhammad, an official in the early community, recalls that Fard had taught her to view Black people as collectively Allāh ("When I would say my prayers, I'd shut my eyes and imagine that great mass of people as god"), and distinguishes between Fard and Allāh.[40]

The Nation of Islam catechism, known popularly as the Supreme Wisdom Lessons, is presented as a series of question-and-answer exchanges between Fard and Elijah, and does not bear obvious signs of later elaboration; Fard, for example, is still referred to in the text as "prophet" rather than "Allāh." The Lessons provide glimpses into the metaphysical and esoteric milieu that Elijah Muhammad inhabited. The Lessons' statement that a white devil who studies Islam can wear the "flag of Islam," but must attach a sword to it, for example, suggests that Elijah Muhammad believed his own vision of Islam to correspond with the secret teachings of the Shriners—which makes it rather striking to see photos of J. Edgar Hoover, who waged covert war against Elijah Muhammad from the 1930s to the 1970s, wearing his Shriner fez.

The Lessons have gone critically underexamined both as a formative text of American Muslim traditions and as an artifact of early twentieth-century American esotericism. The Lessons' concepts of cyclical time and human control over the weather, claims on the true nature of Jesus, references to other religions, use of contemporary racial pseudoscience and eugenics, denial of possible communication between the dead and the living, and rejection of divine transcendence could also place the NOI in conversation with circulating texts, thinkers, and movements of the 1930s.

A few distinct characters emerge in these short snippets of questions and answers. Moses, master conjurer in folk traditions and popular grimoires, appears in the Lessons as a master of "tricknology," the science of deceit and manipulation, which he teaches to the savage white devils in Europe, and through which they ultimately bring bloodshed and destruction to the rest of the world. Moses is represented in the Lessons as a genuine prophet who had been sent by Allāh to civilize white people, but could not properly fulfill his task because he was "half-original" and had lost the knowledge of himself, which caused him to live a "beast life." The Lessons provide an image of Moses as at once a failure stripped of his power and righteousness and also the possessor of a particular knowledge that imposes real power upon humanity.

Besides Moses, another notable character in the Lessons is Yakub, the evil scientist who creates the white race while in exile on the island of Patmos. The particulars of how Yakub went about producing white people most obviously situate the Lessons within the age of eugenics: for a significant period prior to the logical conclusion of eugenics with World War II, the belief that regulated breeding could build a stronger and smarter nation was completely mainstream in American culture. The Lessons, however, provide another element of the Yakub story that usually goes ignored in academic conversation: the moment at which Yakub discovers magnetic attraction and decides to create his devil race. In a short sliver of text, we get a hint of the ideologies circulating around Master Fard and Elijah Muhammad in 1930s Detroit. The Lessons ask, "Who is the founder of unalike attract and alike repel?" and explain that when Yakub was six years old, he played with two pieces of steel and observed that one piece "had magnetic in it" while the other piece did not. Yakub then discovered that the piece with "magnetic" could attract the piece without magnetic. The text connects this moment of discovery with Yakub's subsequent declaration of a "determined idea" that he would someday make an "unalike" nation and teach it tricknology, by which it would come to rule for six thousand years (22:40). Connecting Yakub to magnetism and attraction relates the Lessons to themes that appear throughout New Thought literature and other esoteric texts from the period, including *The 6th and 7th Books of Moses.* During his play with the pieces of steel, Yakub discovers a law of nature that reveals laws of the *mind.* Yakub appears in the Lessons and other NOI literatures as the paragon of metaphysical mastery, both a gifted empirical scientist and supreme occultist. Having mastered the principles of attraction, Yakub becomes the magician who makes reality with his thought. His powers will be matched only by those of Master Fard Muhammad, who boasts of training both in Mecca under the scientist-imāms and in Western universities, and who will take Yakub's nation of devils off the planet by raising up a nation of gods.

Who was Master Fard Muhammad, and what did it mean for him to be Allāh in person? NOI belief in Fard's divinity is often portrayed as a "syncretic" mingling of Islam with the theological backgrounds of Elijah Muhammad and other NOI members, which are treated as essentially mainstream Christianity. This approach often drives the misrepresentation of Fard's divinity as his being an "incarnation" of Allāh. Established churches, however, were far from the only resources in post-migration Detroit and Chicago that could have informed an NOI rethinking of God.

Fard Muhammad was not presented as an "incarnation" of Allāh, because incarnation implies the existence of an unseen, transcendent spirit that decides to occupy a body that is not naturally its own. This is not what happens when Allāh appears "in the person of Master Fard Muhammad," since the NOI denies the existence of an invisible "mystery god." Rather, Allāh *is* a man. Fard Muhammad was trained from his birth in 1877 CE to *become* Allāh through self-perfection and mastery of various knowledges. NOI theology could (and certainly did) use Jesus as a resource for understanding Fard's significance, but this is not exclusively the Christ of established Black churches: it is also the Christ who attains his station via training at the hands of advanced masters in secret lodges, and whose godhood reveals the divine potentials and powers lying within all.

William de Laurence, prolific author, publisher, and distributor of magical goods, was an advocate of immanence theology. His heated criticisms of established Christian and Jewish traditions resonate with the narratives of the Lessons. De Laurence charges that "ministers and priests of religious creeds" have "distorted, counterfeited and destroyed the original teachings of 'The Master Jesus,'" and calls for a liberation of the masses from the ignorance that "Dogmatic Theology, Priestcraft, Creed and Superstition" have imposed upon them.[41] These "original teachings," de Laurence asserts, present God as inherent in all of humanity, and represent not only the true doctrines of Jesus, but also the "Masters of the great schools" in India and the Orient who taught him.[42] De Laurence argues that we can find the immanence of God taught in China, India, and Africa,[43] but that priests have worked to conceal these truths. De Laurence additionally makes the point that Christian Europeans are hypocritical when they pretend to be the most enlightened of humanity while causing destruction and misery throughout the world.[44]

Priests, according to de Laurence, "hide their art" with language of "faith," "belief," and "mystery."[45] As concealers of the truth, they are heirs to those who had crucified Jesus. De Laurence argues that Jesus was crucified for teaching that "God lies within man; that man and God are one."[46] Jesus, he writes, "plainly saw and realized that these rulers, priests and head men were base and unscrupulous rulers and priests, and that they were misleading the people."[47] Jesus stood up against these unjust powers with the simple teaching of what de Laurence calls "knowledge of self": that you are gods, and the kingdom of heaven is nowhere but within you.[48] Just as the priests of Christ's time did everything that they could to eliminate him as a threat and suppress the truth of his teachings, churches today continue to promote "ignorant superstition" to keep the masses under their control.[49] Any religion, minister, church, or lawmaker that takes part in this mental subjugation and fails to challenge the "capitalistic masters" in their "imposition of slavery upon the multitudes," de Laurence charges, is no more than a "fraud on suffering humanity."[50]

The theology and rejection of institutional religion offered by this blond-haired, blue-eyed, turban-wearing white man resonates powerfully with the breakdowns found in the Lessons. In the question-and-answer exchanges between Master Fard Muhammad and Elijah Muhammad, a similar picture emerges. Humanity is divided into three classes: the largest, the Eighty-Five Percent, comprises the masses, who are labeled "deaf, dumb, and blind, slaves to mental death and power" for their belief in a nonexistent "mystery god." The Eighty-Five Percent thus become a contested terrain for opposing forces: the Ten Percent, a class of rich bloodsuckers and slave makers who advocate belief in the mystery god as a means of subjugating the masses; and the Five Percent, the "poor righteous teachers" who reject the Ten Percent and recognize God as the Original Man, the Asiatic Black Man (14–16:40). Like de Laurence, the Lessons present this as the original teaching of Jesus. According to the Lessons, "Jesus's teaching was not Christianity. It was Freedom, Justice and Equality." The Devil uses Jesus to "shield his dirty religion, which is called Christianity; also to deceive the people so they will believe in him" (5:14). For Elijah Muhammad, as with Noble Drew Ali before him, New Thought's assault on establishment Christianity spoke to a long-standing tradition in African American religion: the charge that the Bible of the slave owners was not the "real" Bible, and their Christ was not the real Christ.

After Fard Muhammad's disappearance in 1934, Elijah Muhammad would portray him as an initiated master who had studied under a council of scientists in Mecca to become Allāh. Under Elijah's leadership, the Nation of Islam would develop in Fard's absence as a sort of initiatory lodge whose members developed their own Muslim godhood through study of the Lessons. The construction of Fard as Allāh, and Elijah Muhammad as Allāh's chosen representative, privileged Elijah as the supreme knower in Fard's absence. For at least one thinker in the NOI tradition, the NOI hierarchy would betray the truth within its own Lessons, repeating the failures of Christian churches.

In 1964, a member of the Nation of Islam's Harlem mosque, Clarence 13X, sparked what could be compared to a Protestant Reformation within the Nation of Islam tradition, rebelling against the Nation's hierarchical authority while placing emphasis on the primacy of its foundational scriptures. From his reading of the Lessons, Clarence 13X arrived at the view that if the Black man was God, veneration of Fard as Allāh and Elijah as his messenger was no longer necessary. Discarding his X, Clarence renamed himself Allah and disseminated the Lessons among Black and Latino youth throughout New York, who then studied the Lessons without formal instruction or registration as Muslims at NOI mosques. Through this radical intervention, the once-guarded Lessons were liberated from the NOI's institutional control. In addition, the former Clarence 13X shared his own personal technology to decode the Lessons, his systems of Supreme Mathematics and Supreme Alphabets. And he told his students that they were the "Five Percent" mentioned in the Lessons, the "poor righteous teachers" who would recognize that God was not a spook or spirit and teach that God was truly the Black Man of Asia.

Harlem's Allah eventually extended rights to his title to all of the young men who followed him; today, it is normative for Five Percenter men to name themselves Allah. For its advocacy of personal godhood, Five Percenter culture offers a tremendous amount of internal diversity in terms of views on particular issues (such as the question of whether Five Percenters should consider themselves Muslims, or the inclusion of women or white people as gods), as well as textual sources, traditions, and interpretive methods. While some Five Percenters refer to religious scriptures, speak of their godhood in "mystical" terms, and even claim to influence the weather with their thoughts, others remain resolutely hostile toward anything approaching religion or metaphysics, defining their tradition instead as purely scientific rationality. But even these claims of absolute empiricism and the clear authority of science can provide linkages to thinkers whom we would now term "esoteric" or "occult." Elijah Muhammad's concepts of theomorphic men and spirit's relationship to matter could render him a distant theological cousin of Joseph Smith, prophet of the Church of Jesus Christ of Latter-Day Saints, who himself taught, "God who sits in yonder heavens is a *man like yourselves*."[51] Elijah Muhammad, like Joseph Smith, can be said to have constructed his theology from a "complex cultural amalgam."[52] Much has been said about the variety of sources circulating in Smith's era, including Swedenborgianism, Freemasonry, the hodgepodge of fringe religious movements in upstate New York, narratives that portrayed Native Americans as lost tribes of Israel, and Smith's personal engagements of popular divinatory practices, astrology, talismans, and spirit invocation. In neither case, however, do we end up with reliable family trees, or at least none that can stand alone as *the* lineage.

Today, Nation of Islam and Five Percenter intellectuals often trace alternative genealogies and familial relations. Wesley Muhammad, for example, argues for a kind of NOI Salafism, asserting that the divine anthropomorphism taught by Elijah Muhammad stands in complete harmony with the original Muslim community of seventh-century Mecca as well as traditionalist scholar-saint heroes such as Aḥmad ibn Ḥanbal. I have also encountered Five Percenters who would present their self-deifications as representing the secret essence of Islam, expressed in their understandings of mystics such as al-Ḥallāj and Ibn al-'Arabī. In academic literature, meanwhile, the Five Percenters' alphanumeric codes of Supreme Mathematics and Supreme Alphabets have been repeatedly attributed without grounds to the influence of premodern Muslim groups such as the Hurūfiyya or Arabic *abjad* tables.[53] All of these relationships are drawn retroactively long after the "founder" figures have passed away, and are supported more by surface-level similarities than by any awareness of the founders' actual bookshelves. We have no evidence that Master Fard or Elijah Muhammad possessed any working knowledge of the premodern sources that Wesley Muhammad uses to authorize their theology; Elijah never refers to Ibn Ḥanbal or the ḥadīths through which Wesley Muhammad evidences classical Muslim anthropomorphism. Nor is there reason to assert with any confidence that the former Clarence 13X had embarked on a study of Ṣūfism, let alone obscure movements such as Hurufism that would not have been easily accessible in English sources in the early 1960s; it seems more intuitive to consider numerology within NOI tradition and the non-Muslim numerological resources that surrounded him in American popular culture.

We can easily demonstrate that the efforts of Wesley Muhammad and Five Percenters to reconstruct their traditions' genealogies and relationships are innovative, rather than reflective of the traditions' origins. On the other hand, the creative redrawing of these lines highlights the failure of family trees when mapping links between traditions. If we move beyond the idea of a tradition's origins, meanings, and value as frozen forever in the moment of its founding, but instead think about traditions as being constantly formed and re-formed through the living bodies that engage them, then retroactive genealogies become less of a problem. Someone coming into Five Percenter culture generations after the original Five Percenter community of the 1960s will process its knowledge through different archives than those of the elder gods. Premodern Muslim lettrisms and arithmologies might not have been available or even relevant to the young Five Percenters who comprised the original movement, but in today's community, they offer meaningful bridges for those who want them.

In contemporary Five Percenter culture, we can hear specific vocabularies with roots in Freemasonry and esoteric or occult literatures from generations past, though those meanings have largely faded: terms and phrases like "science," "building," "cipher," "standing on your square," and "magnetic" produce meanings independent of their original world. The "sources" and "influences" of a tradition are always changing, because the tradition itself is subjected to an endless succession of rebirths. Every time that a tradition is read with new eyes, it takes on a new lineage, reinventing its ancestors. When I personally encountered the Five Percenters, for example, I did so as a Muslim whose entry into the culture was opened by its possible relationships to Islam. This informed what I looked for and what I found. When I wrote about Five Percenter tradition, my work produced a new genealogy, consisting of the historical forces and relations that had created my point of access into the Five Percent, my own engagement of the tradition, and whatever new possibilities might result from others reading those/these words.

Alternative Resurrections

Many would refuse to consider communities such as the Moorish Science Temple, Nation of Islam, and Five Percenters as acceptably "Islamic" (or perhaps marginalize them with the condescending term "proto-Islamic"). In the case of the Five Percent tradition, we have the added complexity of Five Percenters disagreeing with each other over whether they should even claim to be Muslims. (Most Five Percenters choose not to.) Relating these traditions to a nineteenth/twentieth-century rise of Western "esotericism" or "occult" revivals could read as a judgment against their Islamic authenticity. This consequence is only possible, however, if we assume that somewhere out there exists an Islam that is completely free of admixture and exchange—an Islam that defines itself only on Islam's terms, a culture-free, history-free Islam that remains shielded from the pollution of non-Islam.

That's not an assumption on which I operate. There is no pure Islam against which we can measure whatever we're marking as impure with terms such as "syncretism" or "bricolage." There is no chance of nonsyncretism or nonbricolage, nothing that isn't already an amalgamation before we attempt to locate its essence. Rather than discredit a group such as the NOI for its historical connections, I would suggest that if we find ourselves surprised by the unexpected hybridities and blendings within one tradition, perhaps we should think about what that implies for *all* traditions.

The history of African American Islam is often written in teleological terms, starting with the destruction of African Muslims' identities in slavery and concluding with a restoration of Islam among their descendants. In these treatments, movements such as the Moorish Science Temple and Nation of Islam are treated as "heterodox" or quasi/pseudo/proto-Islamic rungs on a ladder that leads gradually to "true" Islam. The journey of Malcolm X, who finds Islam through the Nation but performs the pilgrimage to Mecca in his last year and dies as a Sunnī, is seen as the climax and culmination of the Nation's relevance. In these narratives, the death of Elijah Muhammad and 1970s reform of the NOI toward Sunnī universalism led by Elijah's son, Warith Deen Mohammed—which was achieved, incidentally, through a process of textual esotericism in which Warith Deen claimed mystical knowledge of the Lessons' hidden meanings—mark the end of the Nation's meaningful existence.

Such narratives oversimplify complex histories. The notion of African American Islam "evolving" toward Sunnī "orthodoxy" leaves out details such as the Nation of Islam's *growth* after the death of Malcolm X, the post-Malcolm rise of entirely new movements such as the Five Percenters and the Ansaaru Allah Community, the revival of the NOI led by Louis Farrakhan in the 1980s, the continued survival of the Moorish Science Temple, and the largely unrecognized fact that some Muslims perform this supposed "evolution" in the opposite direction—that is, they grow up as Sunnīs and *then* join the NOI, MSTA, or Five Percent. Additionally, if we write with different priorities and investments, alternative teleologies become possible.

Rather than imagine all of these movements and ideologies leading up to Malcolm's reconversion as a Sunnī Muslim and Warith Deen Mohammed's ushering the NOI into a global Muslim *umma*, we could trace the history along different lines. What were the African Muslim identities that had been lost in slavery—did they correspond to a modern articulation of Sunnism and heavily textualized "classical tradition" that would satisfy contemporary leaders such as Hamza Yusuf? Or would popular West African practices of the eighteenth and nineteenth centuries have violated his boundaries of authentic Islam? Certainly, "West African Islam" makes for a category with immeasurable internal diversity, allowing for both classically trained jurists and the makers of gris-gris talismans. GhaneaBassiri suggests that among the African Muslims brought to the Americas, some would have been "religious heirs" to the Muslims condemned as *mukhallitūn* ("mixers") by reformers for their veneration of trees and shrines.[54]

This presents us with a different point of departure, for which the end result is not necessarily neotraditionalist Sunnism. We could instead follow the lines of history marked as "esoteric," "occult," or "magical" and see where they go. African traditions, Muslim and non-Muslim, blend in the American context just as they had in Africa. These traditions intersect with Anglo occultisms, contributing to an American supernatural imagination. Free Black men establish their own Masonic orders and identify with both the glories of pharaonic Egypt and the struggle of its enslaved Hebrews, Moses gets rewritten as a student of African mysteries, Jesus becomes an initiate of Indian schools. Exploring the powers of the mind to transform material conditions leads to new ideas about divinity: Jesus is reimagined as the initiated student who becomes a master, perfecting himself to become Christ and teaching others that the same power rests untapped within them. The concealment of Christ's true teachings by the European churches that claimed to represent him overlaps with the erasure of Black history and tradition by Euro-American slavers. When oppressed peoples discover divine powers within themselves and reject the lies of the slave makers' religion, there is no simplistic division of the "religious" from the "political."

Marcus Garvey, reader of occult "science," imagines future Black religions that can manifest a Black god. Ahmadiyya missionaries, who would be reviled as heretics in their homeland of British-dominated Punjab, call for African Americans to embrace Islam as a return to their heritage and entry into transracial brotherhood—and the Ahmadiyya also present Jesus as an initiate of Eastern wisdom. Noble Drew Ali finds his way into the mystery school of the Egyptian pyramids and emerges as a perfected master, the prophet for his people, bringing forth a new revelation in which all men are said to be thoughts of God and priests unto themselves. Master Fard Muhammad journeys from Mecca to Detroit and denies the existence of God as an invisible spirit-man in the sky; instead, he presents embodied Black humanity as absolute divinity. Fard's student, Elijah Muhammad, presents him as an initiated god who had trained under a council of master scientist-imām-adepts to become Allāh. Elijah's student, Malcolm X, breaks free from the institutional constraints of Elijah's Nation and remakes himself in Mecca; a fellow exile from the NOI asks him if he had seen Fard there. Malcolm's student, Clarence 13X, rejects the Nation's attempt to keep his mind under Elijah's "capture," breaks away from the initiatory lodge of Mosque No. 7, and claims the name of Allah for himself. This new Allah, teaching his own arithmology as a master key to unlock the NOI Lessons on basketball courts and street corners in Harlem and Brooklyn, tells his teen students that they must be their own gods, each of them his own Allah. The Nation of Islam is recalibrated and eventually dissolved after 1975 by Elijah's son, but resurrected by Louis Farrakhan, who asserts that Allāh came to America to show that he could create from nothing with the simple command, "Be!" Allāh-as-Fard came to a people that had been reduced to nothing, Farrakhan teaches, to produce a nation of gods who could manifest their determined ideas in the present world and transform their realities. The whole point of "Islam," in this alternative destiny, becomes the raising of god-consciousness as knowledge of divine self.

The complex histories going into and from the Nation of Islam allow for more than a singular communal telos of blending into a global law-centered umma, as imagined in the Sunnification projects of Malcolm or Warith Deen. The tangling of histories produces alternatives to hegemonic Sunnī globalism as the necessary point of origin and goal of ultimate return. Esotericism/occultism works as a builder of bridges, enabling connections and opening pathways into new milieus—including portals to that Sunnī globalism as a possible future—but also as a dissolver of globalisms and false unities, subverter of imagined orthodoxies even when upholding them on the surface, celebrating the local, the fragmented, and the multiple.

8

Conclusion

> The way we tell it, hoodoo started way back there before everything. Six days of magic spells and mighty words and the world with its elements above and below was made.
>
> —ZORA NEALE HURSTON, *Mules and Men*[1]

The foregoing discussions have attempted to examine traditions and practices that may or may not have been considered "magic" across all historical contexts, but are likely to be perceived as such in our own—with "magic" given a broad spectrum of meanings, ranging from the demonically assisted (but still powerful) to the religiously heretical to mere superstition and the deceptive hustles of charlatans. By no means did I seek to catalog every appearance of a text or practice found anywhere in the "Muslim world" that could be branded as magic, but I believe that thinking about Muslim magics raises important (if uncomfortable) consequences for projects that seek to revive the Islamic spirit.

Writing about magic and Muslims in today's world cannot be politically neutral. Those who would argue that Islam needs to "catch up" to modernity often find their proof in news clippings about accused witches being persecuted under "Islamic law," or Harry Potter books being banned in Saudi Arabia. To many eyes, belief in the reality of magic casts Muslims as stranded at a place of ignorance that the West has long since left behind. Moreover, belief in the inherent backwardness of Muslims feeds into a "white man's burden" or "civilizing mission" narrative that was employed to justify colonialism and continues to accompany the American empire on its military adventures. At the very least, to imagine Muslim traditions as infused with magic—when the readers are non-Muslims and imagine themselves as living in an entirely disenchanted world—threatens to paint an old Orientalist fantasy of Islam as an exotic and strange place "out there" that operates by its own incomprehensible logics.

My approach, then, has been to emphasize the cultural interconnectivity and hybridity present at every stage of Muslim magical histories. There is no point in Islam's history in which Muslims achieved a pure bubble of complete self-definition, isolated from everything non-Muslim. While many Muslims seek to purge their religious lives of non-Islamic influences, I have no idea what such an Islam would look like, because it has never existed. The Qur'ān itself was revealed in conversation with other communities that were contemporary to Muḥammad, sometimes directly engaging their challenges and criticisms, other times simply speaking in the shared language and concepts of their world. While the Ḥijāz region might have been somewhat of a boondocks in the seventh century, it was not on the moon, but located within a triangulation of Byzantine, Persian, and Ethiopian empires and impacted by all of them. As Muslim territorial dominion expanded much faster than Muslim belief, early Muslims in garrison towns of regions such as Iraq lived as minority elites among majority non-Muslim populations; this was the milieu of encounter and exchange in which post-prophetic Islam took shape. The textual tradition of Muslim magic—along with the textual tradition of Islam apart from the Qur'ān, *period*—starts amid the massive 'Abbāsid translation movement, in which Muslim and non-Muslim scholars worked in collaboration to provide the caliphate with a global archive. Muslim practitioners of magical or occult sciences, as well as their opponents, developed their ideas about magic in reaction to deep traditions encountered in Greek, Persian, and Indian literatures. Considering a history of Muslim magic does not further exoticize Islam as an extreme Other to the West or affirm a "Clash of Civilizations" image of East and West, but in fact reveals that drawing these firm boundaries between civilizations, cultures, or even religions betrays centuries of engagement and deep intersection.

If magic is anything, it is deconstructive. It tramples over borders, passes freely between categories, and holds little regard for what we take as concrete walls between religions, nations, or even historical epochs. Magic does its deconstructive work not only between categories but also *within* them, challenging what could be conceptualized as a distinct religious tradition called "Islam," denying its best claims at coherence and historical stability. Where in Solomon's body does the Israelite prophet-king end and the jinn-commanding master sorcerer begin, or at what point do they both make space for the supreme Perfect Man of Ṣūfī traditions? If Jābir ibn Ḥayyān claimed to have learned astrology and letter-based alchemy from the Sixth Imām, Ja'far al-

Ṣādiq, does that make Jābir's knowledge religious rather than occult? Or does it compromise the Imām's *religious* integrity? Magic undoes its own coherence when we are forced to ask what separates magic from religion or science and come to realize that these constructs all stand on perpetually moving ground. Today's science could be tomorrow's religion, or yesterday's magic might have relocated itself as today's religion, or our religions can be rewritten in the rules of tomorrow's science in ways that could make them appear to be different religions altogether. In the imperial science of another historical moment, the conjunction of Jupiter and Saturn not only proved the prophethood of Muḥammad, but established the divinely mandated sovereignty of Muslim monarchs. Today, the Saudi media matrix disseminates literature claiming that contemporary Western geologists and oceanographers and embryologists are baffled at the Qur'ān's miraculous scientific accuracy, even confessing that it could not have come from human authors.

Looking at magic in Muslim traditions reveals just how much editorial work goes into any articulation of "classical Islam" or its "sacred sciences." If we want al-Ghazālī to perform for us as a paragon of Islam's high-end sophistication as an intellectual tradition—that is, a tradition *for* intellectuals—we choose some of him and erase some of him. We might not want al-Ghazālī to share his opinions about magic, if even his rejections of magic remain informed by knowledge regimes of a world that is not our own. As Muslims defending our capacity to be fully "modern," "rational," and so on, many of us point to the 'Abbāsid translation project and all of the great Muslim minds who emerged as shareholders in its legacy. But these thinkers were not only philosophers and empirical scientists as we conceptualize those vocations today:

al-Kindī, considered the "father of Arabic philosophy," also provided articulations of how the stars produced effects on the earth, and how humans with proper knowledge could even attract the stars' energies to fulfill their own needs. In my experience both as a member of Muslim communities and as a teacher of Islamic studies courses at the University of North Carolina at Chapel Hill, I have encountered young Muslims who assert striking confidence in the ḥadīth corpus as a positivist preservation of what "really happened," accomplished entirely by rigorous critical scholarship. What's commonly left out of the Ḥadīth Folk narrative is the dimension that some would call "mystical," others "occult" or "esoteric," today: the extent to which these scholars were inspired and directly informed by dreams and visions. The repackaging of the 'Abbāsid translation project's legacy and the scholarly tradition of the Ḥadīth Folk to satisfy modern needs for scientific rationality depend on cutting out what doesn't fit the narrative. And this process—the marking of some texts, practices, and communities as inauthentic, illegitimate, undesirable, heterodox, alien, and other—is largely the history of how "magic" becomes manifest as its own category.

There's a salient consequence here in terms of power and authority. The question of how we build and package this golden age of "classical Islam" is inseparable from the problem of deciding how we can know "true Islam" and identify the people who are qualified to speak on its behalf. Conceiving a tradition of Muslim magics threatens to present a rival claim on religious authenticity and authority. Allowing for new ways to know things is never good news for the 'ulama, and opening space for new fields of knowledge potentially decenters traditions of jurisprudence, even forcing increased openings for an Islam outside normative Muslim legal traditions. But it was always there; we just don't always see it as part of Islam proper. Rethinking Muslim magics could open the floodgates for a wild new universe of interpretive possibilities.

What do you want the Golden Age to look like? Al-Kindī, *ninth-century occultist*, held that the human soul existed as an emanation from Allāh in the same way that sunlight emanated from the sun.[2] If that feels icky, reconsider: al-Kindī, *father of Arabic philosophy*, held that the human soul existed as an emanation from Allāh in the same way that sunlight emanated from the sun. One more try: al-Kindī, *classical astronomer* (*not astrologer!*), held that the human soul existed as an emanation from Allāh in the same way that sunlight emanated from the sun. If there's a mold in which al-Kindī can be placed that renders him appropriate and acceptable, someone might take those words and fly.

About the Author

MICHAEL MUHAMMAD KNIGHT became a Muslim at sixteen after reading *The Autobiography of Malcolm X*. He is the author of ten previous books, including *The Taqwacores*; *Tripping with Allah: Islam, Drugs, and Writing*; and *Why I Am a Five Percenter*. He lives in North Carolina.

Notes

1

Introducing Muslim Magic

1 Waines, David. *An Introduction to Islam.* Cambridge, UK: Cambridge University Press, 2003. Brown, Daniel W. *A New Introduction to Islam.* Chichester, UK: Wiley-Blackwell, 2009.

2 Hassaballa, Hesham A., and Kabir Helminski. *The Beliefnet Guide to Islam.* New York: Doubleday, 2005.

3 Sfameni, Carla. "Magic in Late Antiquity: The Evidence of Magical Gems." In David M. Gwynn and Susanne Bangert, eds. *Religious Diversity in Late Antiquity.* Leiden, NL: Brill, 2010. 435–476.

4 Dickie, Matthew W. *Magic and Magicians in the Greco-Roman World.* New York: Routledge, 2001. 33.

5 Rose, Jenny. *The Image of Zoroaster: The Persian Mage Through European Eyes.* New York: Bibliotheca Persica Press, 2000. 48.

6 de Jong, Albert. *Traditions of the Magi: Zoroastrianism in Greek and Latin Literature.* Leiden, NL: Brill, 1997. 387–413.

7 Qur'ān 22:17.

8 Graf, Fritz. "Excluding the Charming: The Development of the

Greek Concept of Magic." In Marvin Meyer and Paul Mirecki, eds. *Ancient Magic and Ritual Power.* Leiden, NL: Brill, 1995. 29–42.

9 Bremmer, Jan N. *Greek Religion and Culture, the Bible, and the Ancient Near East.* Leiden, NL: Brill, 2008. 237.

10 Rives, James B. "*Magus* and its Cognates in Classical Latin." In Richard L. Gordon and Francisco Marco Simon, eds. *Magical Practice in the Latin West.* Leiden, NL: Brill, 2010. 53–78.

11 Bohak, Gideon. *Ancient Jewish Magic: A History.* Cambridge, UK: Cambridge University Press, 2008. 78–79.

12 Bremmer, Jan N. "The Birth of 'Magic.'" *Zeitschrift für Papyrologie und Epigraphik* 126 (1999). 1–12.

13 Saunders, Corinne J. *Magic and the Supernatural in Medieval English Romance.* Cambridge, UK: D. S. Brewer, 2010. 17.

14 Yamauchi, Edwin M. "The Episode of the Magi." In Jerry Vardaman and Edwin M. Yamauchi, eds. *Chronos, Kairos, Christos.* Winona Lake, IN: Eisenbrauns, 1989. 15–40.

15 Rose, Jenny. *The Image of Zoroaster: The Persian Mage Through European Eyes.* New York: Bibliotheca Persica, 2000. 42–44.

16 Otto, Bernd-Christian, and Michael Strausberg, eds. *Defining Magic: A Reader.* Sheffield, UK: Equinox, 2013. 42–45.

17 Sizgorich, Thomas. *Violence and Belief in Late Antiquity.* Philadelphia: University of Pennsylvania Press, 2015. 128.

18 Stratton, Kimberly B. "Magic Discourse in the Ancient World." In Bernd-Christian Otto and Michael Strausberg, eds. *Defining Magic: A Reader.* Sheffield, UK: Equinox, 2013. 243–254.

19 Styers, Randall. *Making Magic: Religion, Magic & Science in the Modern World.* New York: Oxford University Press, 2004. 125–126.

20 Ibid., 80.

21 Ibid., 14.

22 Bremmer, Jan N. "The Birth of 'Magic.'" *Zeitschrift für Papyrologie und Epigraphik* 126 (1999). 1–12.

23 Bullis, Ronald K. *Sacred Calling, Secular Accountability: Law and Ethics in Complementary and Spiritual Counseling.* Philadelphia: Taylor & Francis, 2001. 24.

24 Otto, Bernd-Christian, and Michael Strausberg, eds. *Defining Magic: A Reader.* Sheffield, UK: Equinox, 2013.

25 Stratton, Kimberly B. "Magic Discourse in the Ancient World." In Bernd-Christian Otto and Michael Strausberg, eds. *Defining Magic: A Reader.* Sheffield, UK: Equinox, 2013. 243–254.

26 Mol, Arnold Yasin. "The Denial of Supernatural Sorcery in Classical and Modern Sunni Tafsir of Surah Al-Falaq (113:4): A Reflection on Underlying Constructions." *Al-Bayan Journal of Quran and Hadith Studies* (2012).

27 Qur'ān 10:20, 6:59, 72:26, 3:174.

28 Stroumsa, Guy G. *Hidden Wisdom: Esoteric Traditions and the Roots of Christian Mysticism.* Leiden, NL: Brill, 2005. 1.

29 Monod, Paul Kléber. *Solomon's Secret Arts: The Occult in the Age of Enlightenment.* New Haven, CT: Yale University Press, 2013. 3.

30 "Human Odyssey," Facebook group.

2

Magic in the Revealed Sources

1 Ernst, Carl. *How to Read the Qur'ān.* Chapel Hill, NC: University of North Carolina Press, 2011. 157.

2 Palmer, Andrew. *The Seventh Century in the West-Syrian Chronicles.* Liverpool, UK: Liverpool University Press, 1993: 171–72.

3 Schäfer, Peter. "Magic and Religion in Ancient Judaism." In Peter Schäfer and Hans G. Kippenberg, eds. *Envisioning Magic: A Princeton Seminar and Symposium.* SHR LXXV. Leiden, NL: Brill, 1997. 19–45.

4 Ibid.

5 Bohak, Gideon. *Ancient Jewish Magic: A History.* New York: Cambridge University Press, 2008. 81.

6 Mol, Arnold Yasin. "The Denial of Supernatural Sorcery in Classical and Modern Sunni Tafsir of Surah Al-Falaq (113:4): A Reflection on Underlying Constructions." *Al-Bayan Journal of Quran and Hadith Studies* (2012).

7 Lecker, Michael. "The Bewitching of the Prophet Muḥammad by the Jews: A Note a Propos 'Abd al-Malik b. Ḥabīb's *Mukhtaṣar fi'l-ṭibb.*" *Al-Qanṭara* 13 (1992). 561–569.

8 Ibid.

9 Ibid.

10 Ernst, Carl W. *Following Muhammad: Rethinking Islam in the Contemporary World.* Chapel Hill, NC: University of North Carolina Press, 2003. 105.

11 Meyer, Marvin. "The Prayer of Mary in the Magical Book of Mary and the Angels." In Scott Noegel et al., eds. *Prayer, Magic, and the Stars in the Ancient and Late Antique World.* University Park, PA: Pennsylvania State University Press, 2003. 57–68.

12 Dols, Michael W. "The Theory of Magic in Healing." In Emilie Savage-Smith, ed. *Magic and Divination in Early Islam.* Aldershot, UK: Ashgate, 2004.

13 Idem. *Majnūn: The Madman in Medieval Islamic Society*. Oxford, UK: Clarendon Press, 1992.

14 Wolfson, Harry Austryn. *The Philosophy of the Kalam*. Cambridge, MA: Harvard University Press, 1976, 265.

15 Quṭb, Sayyid. *In the Shade of the Qur'an*. Trans. M. A. Salahi and A. A. Shamis. London: MWH London Publishers, 1979. 360.

16 Mol, Arnold Yasin. "The Denial of Supernatural Sorcery in Classical and Modern Sunni Tafsir of Surah Al-Falaq (113:4): A Reflection on Underlying Constructions." *Al-Bayan Journal of Quran and Hadith Studies* (2012).

17 Ibid.

18 Ibid.

19 Francis, Edgar Walter. *Islamic Symbols and Sufi Rituals for Protection and Healing: Religion and Magic in the Writings of Ahmad ibn Ali al-Buni (d. 622/1225)*. PhD dissertation. University of California, Los Angeles, 2005. 63–67.

3

The Force of the Letters

1 Kieckhefer, Richard. *Forbidden Rites: A Necromancer's Manual of the Fifteenth Century*. University Park, PA: Pennsylvania State University Press, 1998. viii.

2 Davies, Owen. *Grimoires: A History of Magic Books*. New York: Oxford University Press, 2009. 3.

3 Ibid., 26.

4 Zadeh, Travis. "'Fire Cannot Harm It': Mediation, Temptation,

and the Charismatic Power of the Qur'an." *Journal of Qur'anic Studies*, vol. 10, issue 2 (Oct. 2008). 50–72.

5 Pormann, Peter E., and Emilie Savage-Smith. *Medieval Islamic Medicine*. Washington, DC: Georgetown University Press, 2007. 146.

6 El-Zein, Amira. *Islam, Arabs, and the Intelligent World of the Jinn*. Syracuse, NY: Syracuse University Press, 2009. 83.

7 Canaan, Tewfik. "Decipherment of Arabic Talismans." In Emilie Savage-Smith, ed. *Magic and Divination in Early Islam*. Aldershot, UK: Ashgate, 2004. 125–178.

8 Mattson, Ingrid. *The Story of the Qur'an: Its History and Place in Muslim Life*. Chichester, UK: Wiley-Blackwell, 2013. 159.

9 Canaan, Tewfik. "Decipherment of Arabic Talismans." In Emilie Savage-Smith, ed. *Magic and Divination in Early Islam*. Aldershot, UK: Ashgate, 2004. 125–178.

10 Pormann, Peter E., and Emilie Savage-Smith. *Medieval Islamic Medicine*. Washington, DC: Georgetown University Press, 2007. 150.

11 Mattson, Ingrid. *The Story of the Qur'an: Its History and Place in Muslim Life*. Chichester, UK: Wiley-Blackwell, 2013. 160.

12 Ibid.

13 Sengers, Gerda. *Women and Demons: Cult Healing in Islamic Egypt*. Leiden, NL: Brill, 2003. 258.

14 Drieskens, Barbara. *Living with Djinns: Understanding and Dealing with the Invisible in Cairo*. London: Saqi Books, 2008. 94–95.

15 Lory, Pierre. "Sexual Intercourse Between Humans and Demons in the Islamic Tradition." In Wouter J. Hanegraff and Jeffrey J. Kripal, eds. *Hidden Intercourse: Eros and Sexuality in the History of Western Esotericism*. New York: Fordham University Press, 2011. 49–64.

16 Brown, Jonathan A. C. *Hadith: Muhammad's Legacy in the Medieval and Modern World.* Oxford, UK: Oneworld Publications, 2009. 48–49.

17 El-Zein, Amira. *Islam, Arabs, and the Intelligent World of the Jinn.* Syracuse, NY: Syracuse University Press, 2009. 210.

18 Drieskens, Barbara. *Living with Djinns: Understanding and Dealing with the Invisible in Cairo.* London: Saqi Books, 2008. 89.

19 Sengers, Gerda. *Women and Demons: Cult Healing in Islamic Egypt.* Leiden, NL: Brill, 2003. 270–271.

20 Drieskens, Barbara. *Living with Djinns: Understanding and Dealing with the Invisible in Cairo.* London: Saqi Books, 2008. 104.

21 Zadeh, Travis. "Touching and Ingesting: Early Debates over the Material Qur'an." *Journal of the American Oriental Society*, vol. 129, issue 3 (2009). 443–466.

22 Wasserstrom, Steve. "The Moving Finger Writes: Mughīra B. Sa'īd's Islamic Gnosis and the Myths of Its Rejection." *History of Religions*, vol. 25, issue 1 (8/1985). 1–29.

23 Madelung, Wilferd, and Paul E. Walker. *An Ismaili Heresiography: The 'Bāb al-Shayṭān' from Abū Tammām's Kitāb al-shajara.* Leiden, NL: Brill, 1998. 69.

24 Ibid.

25 Nguyen, Martin. "Exegesis of the *Ḥurūf al-muqaṭṭa'a*: Polyvalency in Sunnī Traditions of Qur'ān Interpretation." *Journal of Qur'anic Studies* 14.2 (2012).

26 Knight, Michael Muhammad. *Why I Am a Five Percenter.* New York: Tarcher/Penguin, 2009. 164–165.

27 Melvin-Koushki, Matthew. *The Quest for a Universal Science: The Occult Philosophy of Ṣā'in al-Dīn Turka Isfahānī (1369–1432) and In-*

tellectual Millenarianism in Early Timurid Iran. PhD dissertation. Yale University, 2012. 207–208.

28 Stewart, Devin. "The Mysterious Letters and Other Formal Features of the Qur'ān in Light of Greek and Babylonian Oracular Texts." In Gabriel Said Reynolds, ed. *New Perspectives on the Qur'an: The Qur'an in Its Historical Context*. New York: Routledge, 2011.

29 El-Zein, Amira. *Islam, Arabs, and the Intelligent World of the Jinn*. Syracuse, NY: Syracuse University Press, 2009. 82.

30 Wasserstrom, Steve. "The Moving Finger Writes: Mughīra B. Sa'īd's Islamic Gnosis and the Myths of Its Rejection." *History of Religions*, vol. 25, no. 1 (8/1985). 1–29.

31 Canaan, Tewfik. "Decipherment of Arabic Talismans." In Emilie Savage-Smith, ed. *Magic and Divination in Early Islam*. Aldershot, UK: Ashgate, 2004. 125–178.

32 Ibid.

33 Ibid.

34 Fahd, T. "Djafr" in P. Bearman et al. eds. *Encyclopedia of Islam, Second Edition*. Brill Online, 2016.

35 Francis, Edgar Walter. *Islamic Symbols and Sufi Rituals for Protection and Healing: Religion and Magic in the Writings of Ahmad ibn Ali al-Buni (d. 622/1225)*. PhD dissertation. University of California, Los Angeles. 2005. 127.

36 Ibid., 132.

37 Blank, Jonah. *Mullahs on the Mainframe: Islam and Modernity Among the Daudi Bohras*. Chicago: University of Chicago Press, 2001. 172.

38 Schimmel, Annemarie. *The Mystery of Numbers*. New York: Oxford University Press, 1993. 115–116.

39 Zadeh, Travis. "Touching and Ingesting: Early Debates over the Material Qur'an." *Journal of the American Oriental Society*, vol. 129, issue 3 (2009). 443–466.

40 Wasserstrom, Steven M. *Between Muslim and Jew: The Problem of Symbiosis Under Early Islam*. Princeton, NJ: Princeton University Press, 1995. 195.

41 Wasserstrom, Steve. "The Moving Finger Writes: Mughīra B. Sa'īd's Islamic Gnosis and the Myths of Its Rejection." *History of Religions*, vol. 25, no. 1 (8/1985). 1–29.

42 Ibid.

4

The Stars Are Muslims

1 Varisco, Daniel Martin. "The Rain Periods in Pre-Islamic Arabia." *Arabica*, Tome XXXIV (1987). 251–266.

2 Morrison, Robert G. "Discussions of Astrology in Early Tafsīr." *Journal of Qur'anic Studies*, 11.2 (2009). 49–71.

3 Ibid.

4 Asatrian, Mushegh. "Ibn Khaldūn on Magic and the Occult." *Iran & the Caucasus*, vol. 7, no. 1/2 (2003). 73–123.

5 Ibid.

6 von Stuckrad, Kocku. "Astral Magic in Ancient Jewish Discourse: Adoption, Transformation, Differentiation: Asrology and Magic in Ancient Culture." In B. Bohak et al., eds. *Jerusalem Studies in Religion and Culture, Volume 15: Continuity and Innovation in the Magical Tradition*. Leiden, NL: Brill, 2010. 245–270.

7 Ibid.

8 Ibid.

9 Hegedus, Tim. *Early Christianity and Ancient Astrology.* New York: Peter Lang Publishing, 2007. 307–318.

10 Denzey, Nicola. "A New Star on the Horizon: Astral Christianities and Stellar Debates in Early Christian Discourse." In Scott Noegel et al., eds. *Prayer, Magic and the Stars in the Ancient and Late Antique World.* University Park, PA: Pennsylvania State University Press, 2003. 207–221.

11 Ibid.

12 Ibid.

13 Ibid.

14 Gutas, Dimitri. *Greek Thought, Arabic Culture: The Graeco-Arabic Translation Movement in Baghdad and Early 'Abbasid Society.* New York: Routledge, 1998. 1.

15 Livingston, John W. "Science and the Occult in the Thinking of Ibn Qayyim al-Jawziyya." *Journal of the American Oriental Society*, vol. 112, no. 4 (1992). 598–610.

16 Gutas, Dimitri. *Greek Thought, Arabic Culture: The Graeco-Arabic Translation Movement in Baghdad and Early 'Abbasid Society.* London and New York; Routledge, 1998. 1.

17 Marmura, Michael E. "Al-Ghazālī." In Peter Adamson and Richard C. Taylor, eds. *Cambridge Companion to Arabic Philosophy.* Cambridge, UK: Cambridge University Press, 2005. 137–154.

18 Stearns, Justin K. *Infectious Ideas: Contagion in Premodern Islamic and Christian Thought in the Western Mediterranean.* Baltimore: Johns Hopkins University Press, 2011. 16.

19 Motzki, Harald. "The Musannaf of Abd al-Razzaq al-San'ani as a

Source of Authentic Hadith of the First Century AH." *Journal of Near Eastern Studies*, vol. 50, no. 1 (1991). 1–21.

20 Moin, A. Azfar. *The Millennial Sovereign: Sacred Kingship and Sainthood in Islam.* New York: Columbia University Press, 2012. 221.

21 Saliba, George. *A History of Arabic Astronomy: Planetary Theories During the Golden Age of Islam.* New York: New York University Press, 1994. 55, 68.

22 Idem. *Islamic Science and the Making of the European Renaissance.* Boston: MIT Press, 2007. 35.

23 Adamson, Peter. "Al-Kindī and the Reception of Greek Philosophy." In Peter Adamson and Richard C. Taylor, eds. *Cambridge Companion to Arabic Philosophy.* Cambridge, UK: Cambridge University Press, 2005. 32–51.

24 Morrison, Robert G. "Discussions of Astrology in Early Tafsīr." *Journal of Qur'anic Studies*, 11.2 (2009). 49–71.

25 Adamson, Peter. *Al-Kindi.* Oxford: Oxford University Press, 2007. 204–205.

26 Morrison, Robert G. "Discussions of Astrology in Early Tafsīr." *Journal of Qur'anic Studies*, 11.2 (2009). 49–71.

27 Yücesoy, Hayrettin. *Messianic Beliefs and Imperial Politics in Medieval Islam: The 'Abbāsid Caliphate in the Early Ninth Century.* Columbia, SC: University of South Carolina Press, 2009. 124–125.

28 Ibid.

29 Ibid., 126.

30 Colla, Elliott. *Conflicted Antiquities: Egyptology, Egyptomania, Egyptian Modernity.* Durham, NC: Duke University Press, 2007. 86.

31 Yücesoy, Hayrettin. *Messianic Beliefs and Imperial Politics in Me-*

dieval Islam: The 'Abbāsid Caliphate in the Early Ninth Century. Columbia, SC: University of South Carolina Press, 2009. 65.

32 Ibid.

33 Rodriguez Arribas, Josefina. "The Terminology of Historical Astrology according to Abraham Bar Hiyya and Abraham Ibn Ezra." *Aleph: Historical Studies in Science and Judaism*, 11, no. 1 (2011). 11–54.

34 Yücesoy, Hayrettin. *Messianic Beliefs and Imperial Politics in Medieval Islam: The 'Abbāsid Caliphate in the Early Ninth Century.* Columbia, SC: University of South Carolina Press, 2009. 66.

35 Pormann, Peter E., and Emilie Savage-Smith. *Medieval Islamic Medicine.* Washington, DC: Georgetown University Press, 2007. 155.

36 Richards, Edlyn Suzanne. *From the Shadows into the Light: The Disappearance of the Fatimid Caliph al-Hakim.* PhD dissertation. San Jose State University, 2002.

37 Halm, Heinz. *Fatimids and Their Traditions of Learning.* London: IB Tauris, 2001. 86.

38 Ibid.

39 Moin, A. Azfar. *The Millennial Sovereign: Sacred Kingship and Sainthood in Islam.* New York: Columbia University Press, 2012. 11.

40 Ibid., 29–30.

41 Ibid., 116.

42 Ibid., 118.

43 von Stuckrad, Kocku. "Astral Magic in Ancient Jewish Discourse: Adoption, Transformation, Differentiation: Asrology and Magic in Ancient Culture." In B. Bohak et al., eds. *Jerusalem Studies in Religion and Culture, Volume 15: Continuity and Innovation in the Magical Tradition.* Leiden, NL: Brill, 2010. 245–270.

44 Ibid.

45 Ibid.

46 Heath, Peter. *Allegory and Philosophy in Avicenna.* Philadelphia: University of Pennsylvania Press, 1992. 138.

47 Beneito, Pablo. "The Maid of Fourteen: Cycles of Time According to Ibn 'Arabi's Ayyām al-Sha'n." In *Islam-West Philosophical Dialogue: The Papers Presented at the World Congress on Mulla Sadra Religion* (May 1999, Tehran). Tehran, Iran: Sadra Islamic Philosophy Research Institute. 2001. 275–306.

48 Ebstein, Michael. *Mysticism and Philosophy in al-Andalus: Ibn Masurra, Ibn al-'Arabī and the Ismā'īlī Tradition.* Leiden, NL: Brill, 2014. 134.

49 Cattaläy, Godefroid de. *The Ikhwan as-Safa': A Brotherhood of Idealists on the Fringe of Orthodox Islam.* Oxford, UK: Oneworld Publications, 2005. 57–58.

50 Rodriguez Arribas, Josefina. "The Terminology of Historical Astrology According to Abraham Bar Hiyya and Abraham Ibn Ezra." *Aleph: Historical Studies in Science and Judaism*, vol. 11, no. 1 (2011). 11–54.

51 Ibid.

5

Finding Hermes in the Qur'ān: The High Station of Idrīs

1 Fowden, Garth. *The Egyptian Hermes: A Historical Approach to the Late Pagan Mind.* Princeton, NJ: Princeton University Press, 1993. 14.

2 Momigliano, Arnaldo. *Classical Foundations of Modern Historiography.* Oakland, CA: University of California Press, 1992. 32.

3 Cambiano, Giuseppe. "Greek Philosophy and Western History: A Philosophy-Centered Temporality." In Alexandra Lianeri, ed. *The Western Time of Ancient History: Historiographical Encounters with the Greek and Roman Pasts.* Cambridge, UK: Cambridge University Press, 2011. 60–98.

4 Fowden, Garth. *The Egyptian Hermes: A Historical Approach to the Late Pagan Mind.* Princeton, NJ: Princeton University Press, 1993. 14–15.

5 Lelli, Fabrizio. "Hermes Among the Jews: Hermetica as Hebraica from Antiquity to the Renaissance." *Magic, Ritual, and Witchcraft,* vol. 2, no. 2 (2007). 111–135.

6 Ebeling, Florian. *The Secret History of Hermes Trismegistus.* Trans. David Lorton. Ithaca, NY: Cornell University Press, 2007. 30.

7 Ibid., 7.

8 Fowden, Garth. *The Egyptian Hermes: A Historical Approach to the Late Pagan Mind.* Princeton, NJ: Princeton University Press, 1993. 25.

9 Copenhaver, Brian P., ed. *Hermetica: The Greek Corpus Hermeticum and the Latin Asclepius in a New English Translation.* Cambridge, UK: Cambridge University Press, 1995. 41.

10 Fowden, Garth. *The Egyptian Hermes: A Historical Approach to the Late Pagan Mind.* Princeton, NJ: Princeton University Press, 1993. 27.

11 Mussies, Gerard. "Moses." In W. J. Hanegraaff, ed. *Dictionary of Gnosis and Western Esotericism.* Leiden, NL: Brill, 2005. 804–806.

12 Droge, Arthur J. *Homer or Moses? Early Christian Interpretations of the History of Culture*. Philadelphia, PA: Coronet, 1988. 26–30.

13 Ibid.

14 Ibid.

15 Ibid.

16 Deutsch, Nathaniel. *Guardians of the Gate: Angelic Vice Regency in Late Antiquity*. Leiden, NL: Brill, 1999. 35.

17 Ibid., 30–31.

18 Ibid., 44.

19 Ibid., 32.

20 Reeves, John C. *Heralds of That Good Realm: Syro-Mesopotamian Gnosis and Jewish Traditions*. Leiden, NL: Brill, 1996. 39–42.

21 Collins, John J. *The Apocalyptic Imagination*. Grand Rapids, MI: William B. Eerdmans, 1998. 152–153.

22 Deutsch, Nathaniel. *Guardians of the Gate: Angelic Vice Regency in Late Antiquity*. Leiden, NL: Brill, 1999. 59–60.

23 Hamori, Esther J. "Childless Female Diviners in the Bible and Beyond." In Jonathan Stokl and Corrine L. Carvalho, eds. *Prophets Male and Female: Gender and Prophecy in the Hebrew Bible, the Eastern Mediterranean, and the Ancient Near East*. Atlanta, GA: Society of Biblical Literature, 2013. 169–192.

24 Arbel, Vita Daphna. *Beholders of Divine Secrets: Mysticism and Myth in the Hekhalot and Merkavah Literature*. Albany, NY: State University of New York Press, 2003. 98.

25 Ibid.

26 Wasserstrom, Steven M. *Between Muslim and Jew: The Problem of*

Symbiosis Under Early Islam. Princeton, NJ: Princeton University Press, 1995. 190–200.

27 Ibid.

28 Ibid.

29 Ibid.

30 Ibid.

31 Gutas, Dimitri. *Greek Thought, Arabic Culture: The Graeco-Arabic Translation Movement in Baghdad and Early 'Abbāsid Society.* New York: Routledge, 1998. 100–101.

32 Ebeling, Florian. *The Secret History of Hermes Trismegistus.* Trans. David Lorton. Ithaca, NY: Cornell University Press, 2007. 45.

33 Walbridge, John. *The Wisdom of the Mystic East: Suhrawardi and Platonic Orientalism.* Albany, NY: State University of New York Press, 2000. 22.

34 Butterworth, Charles E. "Ethical and Political Philosophy." In Peter Adamson and Richard C. Taylor, eds. *The Cambridge Companion to Arabic Philosophy.* Cambridge, UK: Cambridge University Press, 2005. 266–286.

35 al-Rāzī, Abū Ḥātim. *The Proofs of Prophecy.* Tarif Khalidi, trans. Salt Lake City, UT: Brigham Young University, 2012. 209.

36 Ibid., 210.

37 Walbridge, John. *The Wisdom of the Mystic East: Suhrawardi and Platonic Orientalism.* Albany, NY: State University of New York Press, 2000. 34.

38 Savage-Smith, Emilie, and Marion B. Smith. "Islamic Geomancy in a Thirteenth-Century Divinatory Device: Another Look." In Emilie Savage-Smith, ed. *Magic and Divination in Early Islam.* Aldershot, UK: Ashgate, 2004.

39 Pingree, David. "The Sabians of Harran and the Classical Tradition." *International Journal of the Classical Tradition*, vol. 9 (2002).

40 Green, Tamara M. *The City of the Moon God: Religious Traditions of Harran*. Leiden, NL: Brill, 2007. 6.

41 Ibid., 71.

42 Pingree, David. "The Sabians of Harran and the Classical Tradition." *International Journal of the Classical Tradition*, vol. 9 (2002).

43 Ibid.

44 Walbridge, John. *The Leaven of the Ancients: Suhrawardi and the Heritage of the Greeks*. Albany, NY: State University of New York Press, 2000. 171.

45 Green, Tamara M. *The City of the Moon God: Religious Traditions of Harran*. Leiden, NL: Brill, 2007. 4–5.

46 Ibid.

47 Walbridge, John. *The Wisdom of the Mystic East: Suhrawardi and Platonic Orientalism*. Albany, NY: State University of New York Press, 2000. 38.

48 Green, Tamara M. *The City of the Moon God: Religious Traditions of Harran*. Leiden, NL: Brill, 2007. 137.

49 Ibid., 116–117.

50 Michot, Yahya J. "Ibn Taymiyya on Astrology: Annotated Translation of Three Fatwas." *Journal of Islamic Studies*, 11.2 (2000): 147–208.

51 Ibid.

52 Ibid.

53 Ibid.

54 Peters, F. E. "Hermes and Harran: The Roots of Arabic-Islamic Occultism." In M. M. Mazzaoui and V. V. Moreen, eds. *Intellectual Studies on Islam: Essays Written in Honor of Martin B. Dickson*. Salt Lake City, UT: University of Utah Press, 1990. 185–215.

55 Gutas, Dimitri. *Greek Thought, Arabic Culture: The Graeco-Arabic Translation Movement in Baghdad and Early 'Abbāsid Society*. New York; Routledge, 1998. 104.

56 Baffioni, Carmela, ed. and trans. *On Logic: An Arabic Critical Edition and English Translation of Epistles 10–14*. New York: Oxford University Press, 2010. xvii.

57 Cattaläy, Godefroid de. *The Ikhwan as-Safa': A Brotherhood of Idealists on the Fringe of Orthodox Islam*. Oxford, UK: Oneworld Publications, 2005. 5.

58 Ibid.

59 Ibid, 76.

60 van Bladel, Kevin Thomas. *The Arabic Hermes: From Pagan Sage to Prophet of Science*. New York: Oxford University Press, 2009. 180–183.

61 Ibid.

62 Walbridge, John. *The Leaven of the Ancients: Suhrawardi and the Heritage of the Greeks*. Albany, NY: State University of New York Press, 2000. 52.

63 Bazavi, Mehdi Amin. *Suhrawardi and the School of Illumination*. Surrey, UK: Curzon Press, 1997. 60.

64 von Stuckrad, Kocku. *Locations of Knowledge in Medieval and Early Modern Europe*. Leiden, NL: Brill, 2010. 87.

65 Razavi, Mehdi Amin. *Suhrawardi and the School of Illumination*. Surrey, UK: Curzon Press, 1997. 60.

66 Walbridge, John. *The Wisdom of the Mystic East: Suhrawardi and Platonic Orientalism*. Albany, NY: State University of New York Press, 2000. 23.

67 Walbridge, John. *The Leaven of the Ancients: Suhrawardi and the Heritage of the Greeks*. Albany, NY: State University of New York Press, 2000. 52.

68 Walbridge, John. *The Wisdom of the Mystic East: Suhrawardi and Platonic Orientalism*. Albany, NY: State University of New York Press, 2000. 91.

69 Ibid., 17.

70 Fowden, Garth. *The Egyptian Hermes: A Historical Approach to the Late Pagan Mind*. Princeton, NJ: Princeton University Press, 1993. 182.

71 Brown, Jonathan A. C. *Misquoting Muhammad*. Oxford, UK: Oneworld Publications, 2014. 60.

72 Fowden, Garth. *The Egyptian Hermes: A Historical Approach to the Late Pagan Mind*. Princeton, NJ: Princeton University Press, 1993. 180.

6

Your 1/46th Share of Prophecy: Dreaming Muḥammad

1 Ibn al-Jawzī. *Virtues of the Imām Aḥmad ibn Ḥanbal, Volume Two*. Michael Cooperson, trans. New York: New York University Press, 2015. 327.

2 Donner, Fred. *Narratives of Islamic Origins: The Beginnings of Islamic Historical Writing*. Princeton, NJ: Darwin Press, 1998.

3 Katz, Marion. "The Prophet Muḥammad in Ritual." In Jonathan E. Brockopp, ed. *The Cambridge Companion to Muhammad.* Cambridge, UK: Cambridge University Press, 2010. 139–157.

4 Ghaemmaghami, Omid. "Numinous Vision, Messianic Encounters: Typological Representations in a Vision of the Prophet's Ḥadīth al-Ru'yā and in Visions and Dreams of the Hidden Imam." In Özgen Felek and Alexander D. Knysh, eds. *Dreams and Visions in Islamic Societies.* Albany, NY: State University of New York Press, 2012. 51–76.

5 Maxim Romanov, "Dreaming Hanbalites." Ibid., 31–50.

6 Sirriyeh, Elizabeth. *Dreams and Visions in the World of Islam.* London: I. B. Tauris, 2012. 63–65.

7 Idem. "Dreams of the Holy Dead: Traditional Islamic Oneirocriticism Versus Salafi Scepticism." *Journal of Semitic Studies* XLV/I (Spring 2000), 115–130.

8 Maxim Romanov, "Dreaming Hanbalites." In Özgen Felek and Alexander D. Knysh, eds. *Dreams and Visions in Islamic Societies.* Albany, NY: State University of New York Press, 2012. 31–50.

9 Ibid.

10 Ibid.

11 Dalkilic, Mehmet. "Dream and Spirit in Ibn Qayyim al-Jawziyah's Qitab al-Ruh." In Kelly Bulkeley et al., eds. *Dreaming in Christianity and Islam.* New Brunswick, NJ: Rutgers State University Press, 2009. 137–142.

12 Shaikh, Sa'diyya. *Sufi Narratives of Intimacy: Ibn 'Arabi, Gender, and Sexuality.* Chapel Hill, NC: The University of North Carolina Press, 2012. 2.

13 Knysh, Alexander D. *Ibn 'Arabi in the Later Islamic Tradition: The*

Making of a Polemical Image in Medieval Islam. Albany, NY: State University of New York Press, 1999. 87.

14 Shaikh, Sa'diyya. *Sufi Narratives of Intimacy: Ibn 'Arabi, Gender, and Sexuality.* Chapel Hill, NC: The University of North Carolina Press, 2012. 39.

15 Hidayatullah, Aysha. *Feminist Edges of the Qur'an.* New York: Oxford University Press, 2014. 194.

16 Knysh, Alexander D. *Ibn 'Arabi in the Later Islamic Tradition: The Making of a Polemical Image in Medieval Islam.* Albany, NY: State University of New York Press, 1999. 93–94.

17 Hermansen, Marcia K., trans. *The Conclusive Argument from God: Shāh Walī Allāh of Delhi's Ḥujjat Allāh al-Bāligha.* Leiden, NL: Brill, 1996. 446.

18 Ibid., xxvi.

19 Ibid., 122.

20 Ibid., 64.

21 Sirriyeh, Elizabeth. "Dreams of the Holy Dead: Traditional Islamic Oneirocriticism Versus Salafi Scepticism." *Journal of Semitic Studies* XLV/I (Spring 2000), 115–130.

22 Ibid.

7

Coming of the Black God: Esoteric Revival and American Islam

1 Muhammad, Elijah. *The Theology of Time.* Phoenix, AZ: Secretarius MEMPS Publications, 2002. 26–27.

2 Chireau, Yvonne P. *Black Magic: Religion and the African American Conjuring Tradition*. Berkeley, CA: University of California Press, 2006. 3.

3 Ibid., 3–5.

4 Ibid., 7.

5 Ibid., 43.

6 Albanese, Catherine L. *A Republic of Mind and Spirit: A Cultural History of American Metaphysical Religion*. New Haven, CT: Yale University Press, 2007. 94–95.

7 Ibid.

8 GhaneaBassiri, Kambiz. *A History of Islam in America*. New York: Cambridge University Press, 2010. 67–68.

9 Ibid.

10 Bowen, Patrick. "Islam and 'Scientific Religion' in the United States before 1935." *Islam and Christian-Muslim Relations*, vol. 22, no. 3 (2011). 311–328.

11 Abd-Allah, Umar F. *A Muslim in Victorian America: The Life of Alexander Russell Webb*. New York: Oxford University Press, 2006.

12 Albanese, Catherine L. *A Republic of Mind and Spirit: A Cultural History of American Metaphysical Religion*. New Haven, CT: Yale University Press, 2007.

13 Horowitz, Mitch. *Occult America: The Secret History of How Mysticism Shaped Our Nation*. New York: Bantam Books, 2009. 137.

14 Ibid.

15 Ibid.

16 Styers, Randall. *Making Magic: Religion, Magic, and Science in the Modern World*. New York: Oxford University Press, 2004.

17 Horowitz, Mitch. *Occult America: The Secret History of How Mysticism Shaped Our Nation.* New York: Bantam Books, 2009. 137.

18 Dorman, Jacob S. "'A True Moslem Is a True Spiritualist': Black Orientalism and Black Gods of the Metropolis." In Edward E. Curtis IV and Danielle Brune Sigler, eds. *The New Black Gods: Arthur Huff Fauset and the Study of African American Religions.* Bloomington, IN: Indiana University Press, 2009. 116–143.

19 Horowitz, Mitch. *Occult America: The Secret History of How Mysticism Shaped Our Nation.* New York: Bantam Books, 2009. 125.

20 Polk, Patrick A. "Other Books, Other Powers: The 6th and 7th Books of Moses in Afro-Atlantic Folk Belief." *Southern Folklore,* vol. 56, no. 2 (1999).

21 Horowitz, Mitch. *Occult America: The Secret History of How Mysticism Shaped Our Nation.* New York: Bantam Books, 2009. 141.

22 Dorman, Jacob S. "'A True Moslem Is a True Spiritualist': Black Orientalism and Black Gods of the Metropolis." In Edward E. Curtis IV and Danielle Brune Sigler, eds. *The New Black Gods: Arthur Huff Fauset and the Study of African American Religions.* Bloomington, IN: Indiana University Press, 2009. 116–143.

23 "African Lucky Ring." *Chicago Defender,* July 5, 1924. A6.

24 Dorman, Jacob S. "'A True Moslem Is a True Spiritualist': Black Orientalism and Black Gods of the Metropolis." In Edward E. Curtis IV and Danielle Brune Sigler, eds. *The New Black Gods: Arthur Huff Fauset and the Study of African American Religions.* Bloomington, IN: Indiana University Press, 2009. 116–143.

25 Abdat, Fathie Ali. "Before the Fez: The Life and Times of Drew Ali, 1886–1924." *Journal of Race, Ethnicity, and Religion,* vol. 5, no. 8 (August 2014).

26 Bowen, Patrick D. "Abdul Hamid Suleiman and the Origins of the Moorish Science Temple." *Journal of Race, Ethnicity, and Religion*, vol. 2, no. 10 (2011).

27 Bald, Vivek. *Bengali Harlem and the Lost Histories of South Asian America.* Cambridge, MA: Harvard University Press, 2013.

28 Gomez, Michael A. *Black Crescent: The Experience and Legacy of African Muslims in the Americas.* New York: Cambridge University Press, 2005. 262–263.

29 Joseph, Simon J. "Jesus in India? Transgressing Social and Religious Boundaries." *Journal of the American Academy of Religion*, vol. 80, no. 1 (2012). 161–199.

30 Dorman, Jacob S. "'A True Moslem Is a True Spiritualist': Black Orientalism and Black Gods of the Metropolis." In Edward E. Curtis IV and Danielle Brune Sigler, eds. *The New Black Gods: Arthur Huff Fauset and the Study of African American Religions.* Bloomington, IN: Indiana University Press, 2009. 116–143.

31 Hammer, Olav. *Claiming Knowledge: Strategies of Epistemology from Theosophy to the New Age.* Leiden, NL: Brill, 2003. 147–153.

32 Gregorius, Fredrik. "Inventing Africa: Esotericism and the Creation of an Afrocentric Tradition in America." In Egil Asprem and Kennet Granholm, eds. *Contemporary Esotericism.* New York: Routledge, 2013. 49–71.

33 Wilson, Jeremia Moses. *Afrotopia: The Roots of African American Popular History.* New York: Cambridge University Press, 1998. 81.

34 Gomez, Michael A. *Black Crescent: The Experience and Legacy of African Muslims in the Americas.* New York: Cambridge University Press, 2005. 232.

35 Hammer, Olav. *Claiming Knowledge: Strategies of Epistemology from Theosophy to the New Age.* Leiden, NL: Brill, 2003. 204–205.

36 Horowitz, Mitch. *Occult America: The Secret History of How Mysticism Shaped Our Nation.* New York: Bantam Books, 2009. 136.

37 Ibid., 85.

38 Ibid., 134.

39 Gomez, Michael A. *Black Crescent: The Experience and Legacy of African Muslims in the Americas.* New York: Cambridge University Press, 2005. 278.

40 Muhammad, Burnsteen Sharrieff. *I Am Burnseteen Sharrieff Mohammed, Reformer and Secretary to Master W. D. F. Muhammad . . . and These Are Some of My Experiences.* Detroit, 2011.

41 de Laurence, William. *The Immanence of God.* Chicago: De Laurence, Scott & Company, 1908. 12–13.

42 Ibid., 14, 42.

43 Ibid., 15.

44 Ibid., 36.

45 Ibid., 27.

46 Ibid., 50.

47 Ibid., 85.

48 Ibid., 40, 49.

49 Ibid., 114.

50 Ibid., 116.

51 Albanese, Catherine L. *A Republic of Mind and Spirit: A Cultural History of American Metaphysical Religion.* New Haven, CT: Yale University Press, 2007.

52 Ibid., 139.

53 Miyakawa, Felicia. *Five Percenter Rap: God Hop's Music, Message, and Black Muslim Mission*. Bloomington, IN: Indiana University Press, 2005. 30.

54 GhaneaBassiri, Kambiz. *A History of Islam in America*. New York: Cambridge University Press, 2010. 68.

8

Conclusion

1 Hurston, Zora Neale. *Mules and Men*. New York: Harper & Row, 1990. 3.

2 Travaglia, Pinella. *Magic, Causality and Intentionality: The Doctrine of Rays in al-Kindi*. Turnhout, BE: Brepols, 1999. 42.

Acknowledgments

I wrote this book while also working on my doctoral dissertation, and in more ways than I can say here, this project was possible only because I share my life with the right person. I have more than once boasted in print of the sacrifices that I have been willing to make as a writer, but Sadaf was the real Mick Foley of this show; if the book gets over, the credit is hers.

Writing while a PhD student in the Religious Studies Department at the University of North Carolina at Chapel Hill, I am indebted to my mentors and colleagues there, first and foremost my adviser, Juliane Hammer, who has been both critically challenging and tirelessly supportive. For people who have been reading me over the years: if my work appears to be sharper now than it was five years ago, please recognize this as a trace of Dr. Hammer's training. I am grateful for the mentorship of Carl Ernst, Omid Safi, and Cemil Aydin, all of whom have had transformative impact on my work during my years at UNC. I also appreciate that as a graduate student in this particular department, questions of the constructed divisions between magic, religion, and science first came into my radar through the insightful work and presence of Randall Styers. Finally, I thank my students at UNC. The experience of teaching critically engaged, committed, and passionate students in a frequently hostile environment—a campus at which Muslims and students of color often felt marginalized, intimidated, and endangered, where Confederate memorials stained the landscape, high-profile Islamophobes were invited speakers, and the Religious Studies Department itself was located in a building named after a recognized KKK leader—was personally transformative for me, and has forever informed my sense of what it means to be a writer as well as a member of a campus community. With this in mind, particular appreciation goes to UNC's Muslim Students Association (MSA).

Endless thanks to Allison Cohen at Gersh Agency, a tremendous advocate and conversation partner. A special note of gratitude is owed to Mitch Horowitz at Tarcher/Penguin, whose repeated encouragement has meant the world to me, for again providing this opportunity. I would also like to extend my appreciation to Nita Ybarra, Elke Sigal, and Dave Cole for their contributions to this book's execution.

I should also recognize that as I put words into the world, I am changed by what comes back to me. Thank you to everyone who has reached out after reading my work for what you have added to this conversation.

Index

Ikhwān al-Ṣafā (Brothers of Purity), 128–29
illegal acts, 159
Illuminationist school of Suhrawārdī, 130–32, 134
Imāms succeeding Muḥammad, 147
immanence theology, 183–84
imperial faiths, 28
incantations, 129
India
  and Ahmadiyya movement, 166
  anti-magic laws in, 13
  and Davies' "Evolutionary Tree," 21
  influence on perceptions of magic, 197
  Jesus' lost years in, 173–75, 177, 191
  Muslim population of, 4
Indonesia, 4
Infinite Wisdom (de Laurence), 170
Inside the Gender Jihad (Wadud), 153
intellectuals, premodern, 2–3
intoxication, 52
intro-to-Islam publishing genre, 1–5
Iran, 4
Iraq, 75
Isidore of Seville, 9
Ismā'īlī tradition, 95
Israel, 30, 38
Israelite movements, 166

Jābir ibn Ḥayyān, 71–72, 197–98
Ja'far al-Ṣādiq, 61, 68–69, 71–72, 77, 197–98
Jahm ibn Ṣafwān, 48
Jamaica, 169
Jaṣṣāṣ, Abū Bakr al-, 50
Jesus (biblical)
  and Ahmadiyya movement, 192
  and Eastern wisdom, 174–75, 192
  and Garvey's imagined future, 192
  and immanence theology of de Laurence, 183
  and Lessons of Nation of Islam, 184
  lost years in India, 173–75, 177, 191
  and Nation of Islam theology, 182
  and New Thought, 174, 176
  and slave owners' religion, 184
  and star heralding birth of, 84
  teachings of, concealed, 175, 183, 192
  wise men at birth of, 9, 175
Jevons, Frank, 12
Jilānī, 'Abd al-Qādir al-, 158
Jīlī, 'Abd al-Karīm , 147
al-Jinn, 37
jinns, 36–37
  belief in, 63
  exorcisms of, 63–65
  and Metatron, 120
  possession by, 60, 63–65
  power over, 47
  Qur'ān on, 63
  scholars' views on, 63
  and Solomon, 38
Judaism and Jews
  and astrology, 19, 83–84, 85–86, 105–6
  and "Book of Mysteries," 83–84
  and Catholic Church, 10
  and Davies' "Evolutionary Tree," 20, 22
  de Laurence's criticisms of, 183
  and Devil, 134
  and esotericism/occultism, 19
  and final judgment of God, 123
  intellectual exchanges with Muslims, 75
  and knot-tying sorcery, 39
  and Moses, 113–14

kāhins, 35–36
khamsa (five), 72
Khan, Hazrat Inayat, 166
Khan, Muhsin, 157–58, 162
Kieckhefer, Richard, 55
al-Kindī, 15, 90–92, 106, 199, 200
knot-tying sorcery, 39, 42–43, 45–46

Muḥammad (*cont.*)
- communication with believers, 143, 158
- and disbelievers, 34
- and dream interpretation, 144–45
- in dreams, 137–38, 140, 142–43, 144, 145, 147, 152, 153, 154, 157, 160
- dreams of (prophetic), 161
- exorcisms by, 63–64
- and God's speech, 58, 59
- and *ḥadīth* literature, 16, 89, 146–47
- and historical context of Islam's origins, 29
- and jinns, 37
- and kāhins, 35–36
- Labīd ibn al-Aṣam's bewitching of, 42–43, 50
- on Mu'awwidhitayn, 43–45
- protective practices of, 44, 59
- Qur'ān revealed to, 41, 57–58, 145
- and Ṣābians, 123
- and "Satanic Verses" incident, 79
- and siḥr, 33–34, 41–44, 50, 52
- and spiritualist medium, 165
- on stars and astrology, 81–82, 88–89
- successors of, 147

Muhammad, Burnsteen Sharrieff, 179

Muhammad, Elijah
- death of, 190
- and Fard's divinity, 182, 185
- and Garvey's imagined future, 192
- leadership of NOI, 185
- and Lessons of Nation of Islam, 180
- and Noble Drew Ali's Moorish Science Temple, 178
- and premodern scholars, 187
- theology of, 186

Muhammad, Fard, 178–80, 182, 184, 185, 192

Muhammad, Wesley, 187–88

Mules and Men (Hurston), 195

Muslim Brotherhood, 49

Mu'tāzilī thinkers, 47–48

mystery schools, 170, 174, 175, 192

mysticism
- and dreams, 148, 156
- and European study of religion, 11
- and Ibn al-'Arabī's *Fuṣūṣ al-Hikma*, 154–55
- and Ibn Taymiyya, 153
- and lettrism, 68–69
- magic's boundary with, 17
- and Metatron narrative, 116
- and Shāh Walī Allāh, 155–56
- and Suhrawārdī, 130

Nabu (or Nebo), 124

al-Najm (*The Star*), 80

names of God, 60, 70

al-Nās, 59, 64

Nation of Islam
- catechism of, 179
- and death of Elijah Muhammad, 190
- and death of Malcolm X, 190
- discounted status of, 190
- and Fard Muhammad, 178–80, 182, 184, 185
- and Garvey's imagined future, 192–93
- genealogy of, 187
- and immanence theology of de Laurence, 184
- and Noble Drew Ali's Moorish Science Temple, 178
- and rebellion at Harlem mosque, 185–86
- reform of, 190
- revival of, 190
- status of, as Islamic, 189
- and Sunnī tradition, 190
- Supreme Wisdom Lessons of Nation of Islam, 179–80, 184, 185, 190
- and Yakub, 181–82

Frazer on, 11
instability of, 104–5, 106, 113
intra-tradition collaboration/communication in, 85–86, 106
and science, 98, 99, 101
religion-magic divide
and African Muslims' practices, 165
and Black folk traditions, 164
and development of concepts, 8
dynamic nature of, 198
and European scholars, 12–13
and Hermeticism, 112
and marginalization of magic, 5–6
and Mu'awwidhitayn, 45
and perceptions of authenticity, 19
permeable barriers of, 36
Riḍā, Rashīd, 156–57
Romans, 109–10
rope-tying sorcery, 34–35, 42–43, 45–46
Rosenkreuz, Christian, 170

Ṣābians of Ḥarrān, 123–29
saḥara, 46–47
Ṣaḥīḥ (Bukhārī), 81, 89
sāḥirs, 34–35. *See also* siḥr
Sa'īd ibn al-Musayyab, 52
Saladin, 131, 134
Salafī, 23
Salem witchcraft trials, 164
Sasanian Empire, 7
"Satanic Verses" incident, 79
Saudi Arabia
dream-driven projects in, 157–58
and Harry Potter books, 196
and Hilali-Khan Qur'ān translation, 135, 157–58
and Ibn Taymiyya, 152
Muslim population of, 4
scholars of, 162
and scientific accuracy of Qur'ān, 198
and Sunnism, 152, 157–58
and witchcraft, 13, 14
Schäfer, Peter, 30, 34
scholars
and dreams/visions, 149–56, 158–59, 162, 199
and integrity of ḥadīth, 141–42
and lesser-known intellectuals, 2–3
and Nation of Islam's genealogy, 187
'ulama, 131, 159, 199
See also specific scholars
scholarship on magic, 15
science
in American esotericism, 176
dynamic nature of, 198
Frazer on, 11, 12
magic as related to, 5–6, 11, 198
and magic in late-nineteenth/early-twentieth centuries, 168
and rationalism, 6
and religion, 98, 99, 101
subject to religious challenge, 122
used to back religious narratives, 104
scripturalism, 107–8, 135
scriptures of Islam, 2, 66. See also *ḥadīth* literature; Qur'ān
secrets acquired by jinns, 36–37
Sengers, Gerda, 62, 64
786, power of, 71
seven-tiered heaven, 97–101, 105
Shāh Walī Allāh Dihlawī, 155–56
Shaikh, Sa'diyya, 151, 154
shamanism, 11
Shams al-Ma'ārif (*Sun of Knowledge*) (al-Būnī), 55, 69
Al-Shiblī, 60
Shī'ī Muslims, 3, 17, 67, 128
al-Shi'ra, 80
Shriners, 165–66, 177, 178, 180
siḥr, 48–53
and astrology, 103
categorical parameters of, 52–53
date consumption as protection against, 46